Happy Sizzlein' honey.
You are a wicked awsome cook.
Thanks for makin' me phat!

Love Mona Flo

THE CANNERY

. . . .

Frédéric Couton

THE CANNERY

SEAFOOD

HOUSE

COOKBOOK

Douglas & McIntyre

VANCOUVER/TORONTO

Douglas & McIntyre
2323 Quebec Street, Suite 201
Vancouver, British Columbia
Canada V5T 4S7
www.douglas-mcintyre.com

Library and Archives Canada Cataloguing in Publication Data
Couton, Frédéric, 1962–
The Cannery Seafood House cookbook / Frédéric Couton.

ISBN 1-55365-070-0

1. Cannery Seafood House. 2. Cookery—British
Columbia—Vancouver. 3. Cookery (Seafood). I. Title.
TX747.C68 2004   641.5'09711'33   C2004-901458-7

Editing by Saeko Usukawa and Lucy Kenward
Jacket and interior design by Peter Cocking
Photography by Ron Sangha
Printed and bound in Canada by Friesens
Printed on acid-free paper

The publisher gratefully acknowledges the financial
support of the Canada Council for the Arts, the British
Columbia Arts Council and the Government of Canada
through the Book Publishing Industry Development
Program (BPIDP) for its publishing activities.

CONTENTS

. . . .

· · · · ·

WELCOME TO The Cannery Seafood Restaurant. What began in 1971 as a simple yet elegant restaurant inspired by the fish canneries that dotted British Columbia's west coast has become a Vancouver landmark famous for its fresh fish and breathtaking views.

Located on the south shore of Burrard Inlet, with windows overlooking the busy harbour and the North Shore mountains, the restaurant remains true to its roots. Nautical artifacts adorn our walls, and the freshest seafood graces our plates.

Although The Cannery has always distinguished itself with its seafood, our menu and our food philosophy have evolved during the last three decades. Today, we offer our guests the largest selection of fresh fish in Vancouver, delivered daily from around the world and prepared using innovative cooking techniques. Accompanying the fish is a wide variety of seasonal local produce. The result is carefully prepared and vibrantly presented dishes with flavours inspired by the cuisines of Europe and Asia. We also offer one of the most extensive wine lists in the city, with an emphasis on Old World and Pacific Coast wines, especially those from British Columbia.

At The Cannery, we strive to exceed our guests' expectations. Thanks to the commitment of our employees and our industry partners, we continue to achieve this goal. In these pages, we share with you some of the secrets of our success, so that you can experience a little bit of The Cannery at home.

JEAN TURCOTTE
General Manager

Introduction

. . . .

Cooking takes time. In the past, meal times were not just about eating. They were an important time for the family to talk, to make decisions, to be together. Today, with our busy schedules and hectic lives, we're more likely to fill up on fast food than to take the time to prepare our own food. However, it is more important than ever to eat well.

I've written this cookbook with the home cook in mind. When you eat at The Cannery, we treat you to a wide selection of fish, meats and produce grown on the West Coast or elsewhere in Canada. We tempt you with breathtaking views of Van-

couver plus cold and hot appetizers, soups, main courses and desserts, all prepared with the freshest and finest products available. There's no reason why you can't do the same at home.

All of the recipes in this book can be made in, at most, a couple of hours. By simplifying the presentation or preparing some of the food in advance, you can put together a meal even faster. I've tried to give you the basics to achieve a memorable meal at home, but I encourage you to experiment and come up with your own style.

Being a chef can be very demanding—it takes years of hard work and patience to become one and huge sacrifices of time, energy and commitment when you are one—but food is my passion. I feel fortunate to do a job I love, but it also gives me great satisfaction to pass along my experience, not only to a new generation of chefs but to my customers and friends.

Think about it. It doesn't take very long to prepare good food made with lots of vitamins, minerals and protein. Let's take the time...

Bon appétit!

FRÉDÉRIC COUTON

Acknowledgements

. . . .

WHEN JEAN TURCOTTE, general manager at The Cannery, and I spoke about putting together a cookbook a few years ago, I never imagined that it would take so much energy and running around.

I would like to thank the entire Cannery crew, whose help allowed me to complete this project. My sous chefs, Neeraj Kapoor, Jacques Wan and Eddy Geekiyanage, ran the kitchen while I was working on the book. David Jensen, my assistant, tested all the recipes. Everyone from the front of the house (outside the kitchen) also really supported me and showed lots of enthusiasm for this project. My thanks to Jean Turcotte and Daishinpan, who continue to believe in me.

I also appreciate the hard work of all my suppliers, who understand the importance of quality products. Although I'm not always easy to please, their efforts and extra attention to get the right product go a long way to creating memorable dinners at The Cannery.

Thanks to Grant Wong, for running around during the photo shoot. To Sue Hansen and Mark Rossum, for always trying so hard to get the special fish to me on time. And to Rob Kaleks, Jason Puddifoot, Doug Chase and all of you with whom I work, who make the days interesting. Apologies to those of you I may have forgotten, you know who you are.

I am grateful to Ron Sangha, for your vision as a photographer. To Nathan Fong, for being the great stylist you are. You have an amazing vision of food and you did a great job for the photos in this book!

Special regards to all the chefs with whom I have worked during my travels over many years and across several continents. And to Gilles Dupont, for expanding my view of food and emphasizing my passion for cooking.

Finally, special thanks to Pascale, my wife, and Hugo, my son, for letting me fulfill this passion, which has taken up a lot of our family time. And thanks to my mother, who cooked for a family of eight children. Only now do I understand what a challenge it must have been to cook daily for so many food critics! It is probably because of you that I love cooking so much. You were the first chef I met, and you're still my favourite. Merci.

FRÉDÉRIC COUTON

How to Buy and Clean
Fish and Shellfish

· · · · · · · · · ·

The best place to buy fresh fish is at a specialty fish market. Here are some tips on what to look for.

WHOLE FISH Fish should be displayed on a bed of shaved, flaked or crushed ice that also partially covers the flesh, both to keep it cold and so it won't dry out. Look for fish that is bright and colourful without a bad "fishy" odour or a smell of ammonia. The fins and tail should be flexible, shiny and moist, the meat firm and the gills red in colour. Make sure that the eyes are shiny and clear and that they have not sunk back in their sockets. Fresh fish should be gutted.

Before you buy, ask the fish seller when and where the fish was caught, whether it is fresh or refreshed (previously frozen) and whether it is wild or farmed. You can ask also what variety you are buying, and whether it has a soft, delicate texture and mild flavour or whether it is a larger, gamier-tasting fish.

FISH FILLETS Precut fillets should be displayed in a clean container over ice or covered with tightly wrapped plastic film in a refrigerator case. Look for fillets that are brightly coloured, shiny and moist.

CLEANING FISH

Cleaning fish is a messy job! Most shops will clean fish or fillet them for you, but if you catch your own, the following tips may be helpful.

To clean a whole fish, trim the fins with sharp, heavy scissors. Start by trimming the dorsal fin, then the second dorsal fin and the pectoral fin, if it is a bottom-feeding fish (sole, halibut or flounder). Begin at the tail and trim toward the head.

Next, scale the fish, if necessary (we usually leave the scales on trout, halibut and cod). Place the fish in a sink under cold running water. Using a scaling knife, a large scallop shell or the back of a heavy knife, start scraping from the tail toward the head. The water will clear away the detached scales. Keep scraping until no scales remain on the fish.

To gut a round fish, use a sharp knife to make an incision along the bottom of the fish's body, from its anus to its pectoral fin. Reach into the cavity with your fingers and pull out the guts. Discard them. (The guts of some fish contain roe, which you may want to save for cooking. In cod, red mullet and monkfish, you may also want to save the liver, which is delicious seared in a pan.)

To remove the gills, open the gill cover. Using scissors, cut out and discard the gills, which are very bitter tasting.

Next, use a small spoon to scratch along the red blood line attached inside the backbone. This will release the blood. Rinse the fish under cold running water to get rid of this bitter-tasting liquid.

To gut a flat fish, make a V cut around the head using a sharp knife. Detach the head from the fish. As you pull the head away from the body, the guts will follow. Discard the guts, remove the gills but save the head for making fish stock. Rinse the cavity under cold running water to remove all traces of viscera or blood.

Place the cleaned fish on a platter, cover it tightly with plastic wrap and refrigerate for up to 2 days.

FILLETING ROUND FISH

Place the fish on a cutting board. To fillet a round fish such as a snapper, salmon, trout, grouper or perch, use a rigid filleting knife to make an incision behind the gill. Cut at an angle toward the head until you touch the backbone. Then run the knife along the backbone until you reach the tail. Hold the knife at a slight angle so you can feel and hear it cutting through the bones. Turn the fish over and repeat for the other fillet.

Place the fillets skin side down on a cutting board. Starting from the centre of the fish and working out toward the head or tail, angle the knife toward the belly bones, maintaining a light, smooth stroke. Remove the bones. Repeat until all bones have been removed.

To skin the fillet, place it skin side down on a cutting board. Hold the skin of the tail in your fingers. Using a sharp knife angled toward the skin, cut away from the tail with a delicate sawing motion until all the skin is removed.

FILLETING FLAT FISH

Place the fish on a cutting board, tail toward you and dark skin side up (there is always more meat on the dark skin side). To fillet a flat fish such as a sole, halibut or flounder, use a flexible filleting knife to make an incision along the dark line at the centre of the fish. Cut down to the backbone. Starting at the head and working toward the tail, angle the knife toward the bones, maintaining a light, smooth stroke. Remove the bones. Repeat for the other fillet until all bones have been removed.

To skin the fillet, place it skin side down on a cutting board. Hold the skin of the tail in your fingers. Using a sharp knife angled toward the skin, cut away from the tail with a delicate sawing motion until all the skin is removed.

REMOVING THE PIN BONES

All fish have a series of tiny bones that run the length of their body just under the skin. These are called pin bones. To remove them, place the fillet skin side down on a cutting board. Turn the belly toward you and look for a lateral line that runs from the head about two thirds of the way down its body. If you move your fingers from left to right along this line, you will feel the pin bones. Using a pair of tweezers (special flat-ended fish tweezers are available at specialty kitchen stores but regular needle-nose pliers will work too), pull the bones straight out one by one and discard them.

BUYING SHELLFISH

Shellfish go bad very quickly, so look carefully before you buy them. Shellfish such as clams, mussels, scallops and oysters should be kept in a live tank that is refrigerated and filled with continuously circulating salted water. Buy only farmed shellfish that is identified with a tag or label from the food inspection agency. This tag will tell you specifically when and where the shellfish was harvested. If you buy shucked shellfish, look for clear, shiny, firm and brightly coloured specimens that are refrigerated. Avoid any that are sitting in a pale creamy juice.

Like other shellfish, crab, lobster, crayfish and prawns should be kept in a live tank that is refrigerated and filled with continuously circulating salted water. They will not be tagged. Cooked crab and lobster are available, but I strongly recommend you buy them live and uncooked so you can be sure that they are fresh and healthy. If you must buy frozen prawns, look for firm, shiny brightly coloured specimens that are sitting on ice. Avoid any that have a green discoloration around the head.

Look for shellfish that are active once they have been removed from the tank. They should have a tightly closed shell that snaps when it is touched or when the water in the tank is mixed. As the shellfish age, their shells will start to open—discard any shellfish with open shells, especially if they do not close when the water in the tank is mixed.

When you buy prawns, "21/25" indicates the average number in a pound: in this case, 23 prawns per pound. The smaller the number of prawns per pound, the bigger each one will be.

When you buy scallops, "U" means "under" and "10" is the number per pound, so U-10 means "under 10 per pound." U-10 is a good size for scallops. The smaller the number, the fewer per pound and the bigger the scallops.

Cook and eat shellfish on the same day you buy them.

CLEANING SHELLFISH

To clean shellfish, place them in a large bowl of cold water. Gently mix the water in the bowl with your hand to shake any sand or other debris from the shells. After the water settles, discard any shellfish that have floated to the surface, as these are dead. Repeat this vigorous mixing twice more until the water is clear. Remove the healthy shellfish.

SHUCKING OYSTERS

Most people do not shuck oysters properly. To open the shell smoothly without damaging the meat or crumbling the shell, use a clean cloth and a thin-bladed oyster-shucking knife. Loosely cover one hand with the clean cloth. Position the oyster on the cloth so that the narrow, hinged side is facing you. Insert the blade between the shells as close to the righthand side of the hinge as possible, then carefully and gently slide it around the shell to cut through the adductor muscle that keeps the shell closed. You will have to cut two thirds of the way around the shell before it opens.

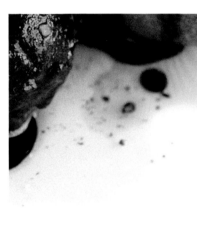

COLD

APPETIZERS

. . . .

I LOVE COLD APPETIZERS

all year round, but especially in the summer.

Often easy and quick to prepare,

they are fresh-tasting and simple.

Take my personal favourite, for example,

a top-quality roe or shellfish marinated with a

little lime juice, olive oil and seasoning.

Tartare of Sockeye SALMON, Scallops
and Beach Oysters

. . . .

SAUCE AND GARNISH

½ cup/125 mL canola, peanut or
    sunflower oil for pan-frying

2 sheets nori (dried seaweed)

1 tsp/5 mL dried wasabi

2 tsp/10 mL water

1 tsp/5 mL liquid honey

½ cup/125 mL soy sauce

TARTARE

3 oz/85 g sockeye salmon fillet

3 oz/85 g scallops

8 beach oysters

½ shallot, finely chopped

2 Tbsp/30 mL chopped fresh chives

1 lemon, juice of

1 Tbsp/15 mL olive oil

1 Tbsp/15 mL lobster oil (page 166)
    or sesame oil

*T*HIS TARTARE RECIPE can be made with any fish, but I really like the flavour of the salmon with the sweetness of the scallops and the fresh saltiness of the oysters. Make sure to mix the fish and seasoning at the last minute, otherwise the salt and lemon will make the fish look like it has been cooked.

Makes 4 servings

SAUCE AND GARNISH: Preheat oil to 350°F/180°C in a deep pan.

Cut each nori sheet into 4 pieces and hold under gently running water for 2 seconds. Pan-fry nori one piece at a time for 30 seconds on each side, until crisp. Drain on paper towels.

Combine wasabi and water in a bowl and mix well. Stir in honey and soy sauce.

TARTARE: Remove and discard skin and grey fat from salmon, then cut into ¼-inch/5-mm cubes.

Remove and discard tendons of scallops (the small white firm pieces attached to the flesh), then cut into ¼-inch/5-mm cubes.

Shuck oysters (page 3), take out meat and chop into small pieces.

Combine salmon, scallops, oysters, shallot and chives in a bowl. Season with salt and pepper. Add lemon juice, olive oil and lobster oil, then toss gently. Let sit for 1 minute.

TO SERVE: Divide tartare mixture among individual plates and add a drop or more of sauce to each. Garnish with nori chips.

Fresh Beach OYSTERS
with Lemon Crème Fraîche

. . . .

*T*HIS IS a very simple way to eat oysters. On the West Coast, we have about twenty different varieties of oysters, including such favourites as Fanny Bay, Royal Miyagi, Kushi, Golden Mantle or Harmony Bay Beach, but for this recipe I use small beach oysters.

Makes 4 servings

Combine whipping cream and buttermilk in a bowl. Cover and leave at room temperature for 30 hours. The cream will thicken.

Strain lemon juice and stir into the cream mixture. Add the sour cream. Add chives and Tabasco. Cover and refrigerate crème fraîche until needed.

TO SERVE: Decorate a serving tray with a bed of seaweed. Shuck oysters (page 3) and discard the tops of the shells. Detach the oysters but leave them in the bottom shells and arrange on the seaweed. Serve the crème fraîche in a small bowl on the side.

1 cup/250 mL whipping cream

¼ cup/60 mL buttermilk

½ lemon, juice of

2 Tbsp/30 mL sour cream

2 Tbsp/30 mL chopped fresh chives

½ tsp/2.5 mL Tabasco, or to taste

1 lb/450 g fresh cleaned
   beach seaweed

24 beach oysters

Poached SPOT PRAWNS
with Lobster Oil Mayonnaise
. . . .

MAYONNAISE

1 cup/250 mL vegetable oil

½ cup/125 mL lobster oil (page 166)
  or olive oil or sesame oil

2 egg yolks

1 Tbsp/15 mL Dijon mustard

1 Tbsp/15 mL water

½ lemon, juice of

¼ tsp/1 mL sambal oelek, or to taste

2 cloves garlic, chopped

PRAWNS

8 cups/2 L court bouillon (page 163)

2 lbs/900 g fresh spot prawns
  (about 70)

*T*HIS IS A GREAT DISH for summer parties because you can eat it with your fingers!

Spot prawns are a Pacific delicacy and are best when fresh. If you buy directly from the boat, pack them in a cooler and cover them with crushed ice. You can also find spot prawns frozen, either in small containers or in a block. Although you can use prawns with the heads removed, I buy prawns with the heads still on because I love their flavour. To thaw prawns, place them in a bowl and refrigerate them overnight. Cook them quickly afterward, since spot prawns tend to turn black after a day in the refrigerator.

You can use this same recipe with other varieties of prawns, such as green, pink or black tiger.

Makes 4 servings

MAYONNAISE: Combine vegetable oil and lobster oil in a bowl. In another bowl, whisk together egg yolks and Dijon mustard. While whisking, slowly add enough of the combined oils to get a thick consistency. Whisk in water. Keep whisking and slowly add the remaining combined oils, lemon juice, sambal oelek and garlic. Season to taste with salt and pepper. Cover and refrigerate until needed.

PRAWNS: Place court bouillon in a large saucepan on high heat and bring to a boil. Cook for 10 minutes. Add prawns, bring back to a boil and poach for 2½ minutes. Drain prawns, discarding court bouillon and any solids. Allow the prawns to cool for 30 minutes.

TO SERVE: Place prawns in a bowl and serve with mayonnaise on the side.

Sockeye Salmon CARPACCIO

Marinated with Lime and Olive Oil

. . . .

CARPACCIO CAN BE MADE with tuna, beef, lamb, scallops, spot prawns or even portobello mushrooms. Fish carpaccio must be made with very fresh fish. Let your fish supplier know what you are making to ensure you get the freshest product available. To thinly slice the salmon, place the fillet in the freezer for a couple of hours then cut the salmon lengthwise with a sharp knife.

If pea shoots are not available, substitute additional radish sprouts or sunflower sprouts.

Makes 4 servings

Remove and discard skin and grey fat from salmon. Cut salmon into very thin slices and arrange on a large chilled serving platter.

Combine lime juice and 1 Tbsp/15 mL of the olive oil in a bowl. Brush oil mixture over salmon slices and sprinkle with fleur de sel, freshly ground black pepper, celery leaves, chives and red onion. Let sit for 1 minute.

In another bowl, toss together radish sprouts, sunflower sprouts, pea shoots and the remaining olive oil.

TO SERVE: Arrange salad mixture in a mound on top of salmon slices. Serve immediately.

1 lb/450 g sockeye salmon fillet
   in one piece, pin bones removed
   (page 2)

1 lime, juice of

2 Tbsp/30 mL extra-virgin olive oil

1 tsp/5 mL fleur de sel

1 tsp/5 mL chopped young
   celery leaves

1 tsp/5 mL chopped chives

1 tsp/5 mL finely chopped red onion

½ cup/125 mL radish sprouts

½ cup/125 mL sunflower sprouts

½ cup/125 mL pea shoots

Roasted TOMATOES with
Aged Balsamic Vinegar and Extra-Virgin Olive Oil
on Toasted Country Bread

. . . .

8 cherry tomatoes

3 Tbsp/45 mL extra-virgin olive oil

2 cloves garlic, chopped

4 slices country or ciabatta bread

3 Tbsp/45 mL 5-year-old
    balsamic vinegar

8 bay leaves

*T*HIS COMFORT FOOD is quick to prepare and very tasty, and it works well as a tapas dish. If you don't have 5-year-old balsamic vinegar, you can use a balsamic reduction. Heat ½ cup/125 mL balsamic vinegar in a saucepan over medium heat. Reduce it to a third, about 5 minutes, then keep at room temperature until needed.

Makes 4 servings

Preheat the oven to 400°F/200°C. Use a small knife to make a cut on the top of each tomato. Sprinkle with salt and pepper and 1 Tbsp/15 mL of the olive oil. Place tomatoes in a roasting pan and roast in the oven for about 6 minutes, until soft. Remove the tomatoes from the oven, transfer them to a plate and allow to cool for a few minutes, then chill in the refrigerator for 2 hours.

Preheat the oven to 375°F/190°C. Combine garlic and 1 Tbsp/ 15 mL of the olive oil in a bowl. Brush mixture onto both sides of bread slices. Place bread on a cookie sheet and toast each side in the oven for about 6 minutes, until golden on both sides.

TO SERVE: Arrange the toasts on a large colourful serving platter. Place a cold tomato on each slice of toast. Drizzle with the remaining olive oil and balsamic vinegar. Garnish with bay leaves.

Seafood SALAD, South Asian–style

. . . .

*T*HIS IS A NICE REFRESHING SALAD on a hot summer day. Use whatever shellfish you can find at the market or substitute fresh fish such as snapper, salmon, tuna or sole. Just cut the fish into small cubes and cook them a bit longer than you would the shellfish.

Makes 4 servings

BOUQUET GARNI: On an 8 × 8-inch/20 × 20-cm piece of cheesecloth, place parsley, thyme, bay leaves, celery and leek. Gather the corners of the cheesecloth and tie together with string.

SEAFOOD SALAD: Wash clams well. Wash mussels, making sure to remove and discard their beards. Remove tendons from scallops (the small white firm pieces attached to the flesh). Remove and discard shells from prawns, then devein. Clean and cut squid into strips.

Cut tomatoes into quarters, then remove and discard seeds. Slice tomato flesh into thin strips. Place tomatoes, cucumber, celery, green onions and red onion in a bowl.

Place glass noodles in another bowl and cover with boiling water. Stir in ½ tsp/2.5 mL of the salt and let sit for 10 minutes. Drain noodles through a sieve and place in a serving bowl to cool. When cool, add sliced vegetables.

Fill a saucepan three quarters full of water and bring to a boil on high heat. Add bouquet garni, the remaining salt and 1 tsp/ 5 mL of the ginger. Cook for 2 minutes. Add clams and mussels, cover the pot with a lid and cook for 20 seconds. Add scallops, prawns and squid, cover the pot with a lid and cook for 1 minute, until clams and mussels open.

Drain shellfish in a colander and discard bouquet garni. Cool down shellfish for 1 minute under cold running water, then drain on paper towels. Add to the bowl of glass noodles and sliced vegetables.

Make a dressing by combining lime juice, the remaining ginger, chili pepper, sesame oil, vegetable oil, honey, sugar and oyster sauce.

TO SERVE: Pour dressing over salad, add chopped mint and cilantro, then toss gently. Season to taste with salt and pepper. Sprinkle with toasted sesame seeds and baby shrimp. Garnish with sprigs of mint and cilantro.

BOUQUET GARNI

8 sprigs fresh parsley

2 sprigs fresh thyme

3 bay leaves

2 pieces celery, each 4 inches/10 cm

½ leek, white part only

SEAFOOD SALAD

8 Manila clams

8 mussels

4 scallops

4 prawns, size 21/25 (page 3)

2 oz/60 g squid

2 tomatoes

½ long English cucumber, deseeded and julienned

1 stalk celery, julienned

2 green onions, julienned

½ red onion, finely sliced

½ lb/225 g glass noodles

1½ tsp/7.5 mL salt

2 tsp/10 mL julienned fresh ginger

2 limes, juice of

½ red Thai chili pepper, chopped

2 Tbsp/30 mL sesame oil

1 Tbsp/15 mL vegetable oil

1 Tbsp/15 mL honey

1 Tbsp/15 mL sugar

1 Tbsp/15 mL oyster sauce

1 Tbsp/15 mL fresh chopped mint

1 Tbsp/15 mL chopped fresh cilantro

1 tsp/5 mL toasted sesame seeds

2 oz/60 g baby shrimp

1 Tbsp/15 mL sprigs mint for garnish

5 sprigs fresh cilantro for garnish

Smoked Salmon and Pickled
CUCUMBER in a Vietnamese Salad Roll
with Tamarind Sauce

. . . .

SAUCE

½ cup/125 mL dried tamarind

2 cups/500 mL water

2 Tbsp/30 mL brown sugar

½ tsp/2.5 mL sambal oelek,
  or to taste

1½ tsp/7.5 mL cornstarch

1½ tsp/7.5 mL cold water

SALAD ROLL

½ long English cucumber, peeled
  and deseeded

½ cup/125 mL rice vinegar

1 Tbsp/15 mL pickled ginger

½ cup/125 mL chopped fresh cilantro

4 oz/115 g mesclun or micro greens
  (about 4 cups/1 L)

2 Tbsp/30 mL chopped fresh mint

1 Tbsp/15 mL sesame oil

6 sheets of round rice paper, each
  8 inches/20 cm in diameter

12 slices smoked salmon

24 chives for garnish

1 Tbsp/15 mL chopped fresh
  cilantro for garnish

*T*HE IDEA for this salad roll recipe came from Hoa Chung, who makes our cold appetizers and helps prepare our salads, vinaigrettes and pastries. It is a nice healthy alternative to a sandwich at lunch, and it can be garnished with crabmeat, shrimp, chicken salad or vegetables.

Makes 6 servings

SAUCE: To make tamarind paste, place tamarind and 2 cups/500 mL water in a bowl and let soak for 2 hours. Place tamarind and soaking water in a saucepan on low heat. Stir in brown sugar and sambal oelek, then cook for 20 minutes until the mixture becomes a paste. In a small bowl, combine cornstarch and cold water. Slowly add cornstarch mixture to tamarind paste and cook for 2 minutes. Strain through a sieve and allow to cool.

SALAD ROLL: After you put the tamarind to soak, cut cucumber into long thin strips and place in a shallow dish. Add rice vinegar, pickled ginger and a pinch of salt. Allow to marinate for 2 hours. Strain cucumber through a sieve and discard the marinade. Drain cucumber on paper towels.

Toss cilantro with mesclun, mint, sesame oil and a pinch of salt in a bowl.

Soak one sheet of rice paper in a dish of warm water for 20 seconds until soft, then place on a cutting board. Place a sixth of the mesclun mixture in a vertical row down the middle of the rice paper. Add two slices of smoked salmon and a few strips of marinated cucumber. Fold down top of rice paper, fold up bottom, fold left side over the filling and then roll up.

TO SERVE: Cut the salad rolls in half, then cut those pieces in half at an angle. Lay the rolls on a serving platter. Garnish with chives and cilantro. Pour tamarind sauce around.

Layered Mediterranean VEGETABLES
with Tomato Vinaigrette

. . . .

1 clove garlic

1 Tbsp/15 mL chopped fresh parsley

1 Tbsp/15 mL chopped fresh basil

¼ cup/60 mL extra-virgin olive oil

1 red bell pepper, deseeded
    and halved

½ green bell pepper, deseeded

½ yellow bell pepper, deseeded

1 small zucchini

1 small Japanese eggplant

2 Tbsp/30 mL chopped pitted
    niçoise olives

½ cup/125 mL fresh basil leaves

¼ cup/60 mL tomato vinaigrette
    (page 166)

*F*OR VEGETARIANS, this is a flavourful, visually appealing summer dish that can be made with any vegetables. If you don't have a barbecue you can still make this appetizer—just sauté the vegetables in a nonstick pan and transfer them to an ovenproof tray. Finish cooking the vegetables in a 400°F/200°C oven, until soft.

Makes 4 servings

Preheat the oven to 375°F/190°C. Line a terrine pan 6 × 1¾ inches/ 15 × 4.5 cm with plastic wrap, making sure there is enough hanging outside the pan to cover the terrine later. Smooth well along the edges.

Place garlic, parsley, chopped basil, olive oil, salt and freshly ground black pepper in a blender. Mix for 1 minute on medium speed.

Slice the red, green and yellow bell peppers lengthwise into strips 1 inch/2.5 cm wide. Use a Japanese mandoline to cut zucchini and eggplant lengthwise into strips ⅛ inch/3 mm thick. Place peppers, zucchini and eggplant in a large bowl, then add the olive oil mixture, salt and pepper to taste, and toss gently. Place the vegetables on a grill pan on medium heat for 2 minutes per side, until tender. Finish cooking peppers in a roasting pan in the oven for 7 minutes, until soft.

Arrange the grilled vegetables in the terrine pan in layers, starting with some of the zucchini, then olives, basil leaves, pepper and eggplant. Repeat process until all the vegetables are used. Fold the plastic wrap over the terrine and place a weight of 2 lbs/900 g on top of it to press down the contents. Refrigerate for 5 hours. The terrine will keep in the fridge for up to 3 days.

TO SERVE: Open the plastic wrap and turn the terrine upside down on a cutting board. Tug gently on the plastic film to release the terrine from the pan. Warm a knife blade under hot running water and cut the terrine into slices 1½ inch/3 cm thick.

Place a slice on each chilled plate and drizzle a small amount of the tomato vinaigrette on the side for a nice colour contrast.

Cured Quebec FOIE GRAS with
Smoked Goose Breast

. . . .

*T*HIS IS A VERY TRADITIONAL and flavourful dish that originated in the south of France, where foie gras has been a delicacy since the days of the Roman Empire. Nowadays, it takes 13 to 21 days of feeding a bird with corn and grain two or three times daily to make foie gras. Most foie gras comes from France, Israel, Eastern Europe, California and Quebec, which is where we get ours. I prefer duck foie gras over the goose variety. A duck liver averages around 450 to 550 grams.

Makes 8 servings

FOIE GRAS: Combine sherry vinegar, cider vinegar, pickling salt and water in a bowl. Place foie gras in the mixture, cover and marinate in the refrigerator for 24 hours.

SALAD: Preheat the oven to 350°F/180°C. Place walnuts on a cookie sheet and toast in the oven for 8 minutes. Do not overcook or walnuts will become bitter. Transfer nuts to a plate and allow to cool.

To make the dressing, place sherry vinegar and Dijon mustard in a blender. Mix for 20 seconds. With the blender running, slowly add hazelnut oil. Season to taste with salt and pepper.

Place smoked goose in a serving bowl with lettuce leaves and toasted walnuts. Add dressing and toss gently.

Remove cured foie gras from the marinade and drain on paper towels. Discard the marinade. Warm a thin knife blade in hot water and thinly slice foie gras. It is very important to warm the knife in hot water to help slice the foie gras cleanly.

TO SERVE: Arrange foie gras slices on the salad and garnish with chervil.

FOIE GRAS

2 cups/500 mL sherry vinegar

1 cup/250 mL cider vinegar

1 Tbsp/15 mL pickling salt

6 cups/1.5 L cold water

1 lb/450 g fresh duck foie gras

SALAD

½ cup/125 mL walnuts

3 Tbsp/45 mL sherry vinegar

1 Tbsp/15 mL Dijon mustard

3 Tbsp/45 mL hazelnut oil or
    walnut oil or olive oil

1 smoked goose breast, 7 oz/
    200 g, thinly sliced,
    or smoked duck breast

1 large frisée lettuce

½ cup/125 mL fresh chervil for
    garnish

SCALLOP Carpaccio with Ginger–Lemon Grass Oil and Tobiko

. . . .

WE GET very nice fresh scallops from Vancouver Island; however, they can be pricey. If you can't find fresh scallops, you can use frozen ones. Try to find FAS (frozen at sea) scallops, which have a far superior quality.

Shiso is a Japanese herb (also called oba, Japanese basil, perilla or beefsteak plant) that is part of the basil and mint family. The aromatic leaves have a very delicate flavour of pepper and lemon, and are used for a tasty garnish. If shiso is not available, you can substitute cilantro or young celery leaves.

Makes 4 servings

Peel and thinly slice ginger. Place ginger, lemon grass and vegetable oil in a blender and mix for 1 minute. Transfer to a bowl, cover and refrigerate overnight. Strain through a sieve into a bowl.

Remove and discard tendons of scallops (the small white firm pieces attached to the flesh). Cut scallops into very thin slices and arrange around the edge of a chilled serving platter.

Strain lemon juice through a sieve. Add strained juice and pickled ginger to the fresh ginger mixture. Brush mixture over scallops, then season to taste with salt and pepper.

TO SERVE: Toss watercress and sesame oil together in a bowl, then season to taste with salt and pepper. Place in the middle of the platter of scallops, then sprinkle with tobiko and cilantro. Garnish with shiso.

¼ cup/60 mL fresh ginger
(3-inch/7.5-cm piece)
½ stalk lemon grass, thinly sliced
¼ cup/60 mL vegetable oil
10 oz/285 g scallops
1 lemon, juice of
2 Tbsp/30 mL pickled ginger
1 bunch watercress, leaves only
1 tsp/5 mL sesame oil
1 Tbsp/15 mL tobiko (flying fish roe)
1 Tbsp/15 mL chopped fresh cilantro
4 fresh shiso leaves for garnish

Ahi TUNA Gravlax Accented
with Green Cardamom and Chuka Salad

. . . .

2 lbs/900 g fillet Ahi tuna,
    preferably a centre cut

2 cups/500 mL fresh dill

2 Tbsp/30 mL green cardamom

1 cup/250 mL brown sugar

2 cups/500 mL pickling salt

2 Tbsp/30 mL crushed black pepper

¼ cup/60 mL cognac

⅓ cup/75 mL extra-virgin olive oil

1 cup/250 mL chuka wakame
    (seaweed salad) or mixed
    sprout salad

1 Tbsp/15 mL chopped fresh dill
    for garnish

2 Tbsp/30 mL soy sauce

*A*HI TUNA is a good choice for gravlax because of its firm texture. I do not use albacore because the meat is too soft, or tombo because its flavour is too mild. Salmon or sea bass are also good choices for this recipe. Gravlax can be kept in the freezer for a couple of days. However, make sure it is well wrapped and air tight.

Wakame is a seaweed that is often added to soups and salads. Chuka wakame is a salad made from wakame marinated with sesame oil, pepper, salt and vinegar. It is a product from Japan and California and is mainly used in Japanese cuisine.

Makes 4 to 6 servings

Cut tuna lengthwise so that it is 1 inch/2.5 cm thick and 4 inches/ 10 cm wide. Save the trimmed-off tuna for use in another recipe such as a bouillabaisse or a seafood salad.

Cut off and discard the big stems from dill. Put 1 cup aside for garnish and finely chop all of the remaining dill, including the small stems.

Place green cardamom in a spice mill (or a clean coffee grinder) and grind into a powder. Set aside 1 tsp/5 mL of the ground cardamom.

Combine chopped dill, the rest of the ground cardamom, brown sugar, pickling salt and crushed black pepper in a deep pan. Spread a third of this salt mixture on a large plate and place tuna on it. Cover tuna with the remaining salt mixture. Pour cognac evenly over tuna. Cover and refrigerate for 2 hours.

Scrape off but do not discard the salt mixture from the top of the tuna. Turn the tuna over. Mix the scraped-off salt mixture well, then cover tuna with it. Cover and refrigerate for 2 hours.

Scrape off and discard the salt mixture from tuna. Gently rinse tuna under cold running water, then drain on paper towels.

Chop the remaining 1 cup/250 mL dill and mix with the reserved 1 tsp/5 mL of ground cardamom in a bowl. Stir in olive oil. Spread half of this mixture on a piece of plastic wrap about 10 × 12 inches/ 25 × 30 cm. Place tuna on it and cover with the remaining mixture. Wrap the plastic wrap around the tuna and place on a cookie sheet. Place another cookie sheet on top of the tuna, and, on top of that,

place a 1-pound/450-g weight. Refrigerate overnight. A couple of hours before serving, place the fillet in the freezer.

TO SERVE: Cut the chilled tuna into paper-thin slices. Arrange 4 to 6 slices of tuna on each plate, then spoon 2 Tbsp/30 mL of the chuka wakame into the middle of each plate. Sprinkle with dill, then drizzle with a few drops of soy sauce.

HOT

APPETIZERS

. . . .

OUR HOT APPETIZERS

are all made from local ingredients. You can buy these

seafood products in season at the market.

If you plan to catch your own fish or shellfish,

just check with the fisheries and health

departments before you go, to be sure the fish

are plentiful and safe for eating.

Deep-fried SEA CUCUMBER
with Warm Tomato Vinaigrette
and Sea Asparagus

. . . .

VINAIGRETTE

½ cup/125 mL extra-virgin olive oil

1 shallot, sliced

1 clove garlic, sliced

1 tsp/5 mL tomato paste

3 Roma tomatoes, quartered

¼ cup/60 mL balsamic vinegar

1 Tbsp/15 mL chopped fresh basil

SEA CUCUMBERS AND
SEA ASPARAGUS

8 cups/2 L vegetable oil for deep-
   frying

6 oz/170 g sea cucumbers, cleaned
   (no skin and no membrane)

1 egg

¼ cup/60 mL milk

⅓ cup/75 mL all-purpose flour

½ cup/125 mL panko (Japanese
   bread crumbs) (page 39)

4 cups/1 L warm water

1 tsp/5 mL salt

1 cup/250 mL fresh sea asparagus
   (page 63)

1 tsp/5 mL chopped fresh basil
   for garnish

SEA CUCUMBERS are long cucumber-shaped marine animals, available in Chinese or Japanese food stores. They are a delicacy among First Nations peoples and in Asia; however, most North Americans avoid them. All of the more than 650 species have strong muscles the length of their body, so it is best to cut them crosswise into rings. Sauté the rings quickly in a wok, being careful not to overcook them or they will become rubbery. Use them also in sea-food salads.

Makes 4 servings

VINAIGRETTE: Heat 1 Tbsp/15 mL of the olive oil in a saucepan on medium heat. Sauté shallot and garlic for 2 minutes, until shallot becomes translucent. Stir in tomato paste and cook for 1 minute. Add tomato quarters, then turn down the heat to low and cook for 15 minutes. Stir in balsamic vinegar and cook for 1 minute.

Transfer contents to a blender or food processor and mix well. With the motor running, slowly add the remaining olive oil and basil. Season to taste with salt and pepper. Keep warm.

SEA CUCUMBERS AND SEA ASPARAGUS: Preheat oil in a deep fryer to 350°F/180°C. Cut sea cucumber into rings 2 inches/5 cm wide, then cut each ring into strips 3 inches/7.5 cm long.

In one bowl, combine egg, milk, and salt and pepper to taste. Place flour and panko in two separate bowls. Roll each sea cucumber strip in flour, dip in egg mixture and finish by rolling in panko, making sure to coat it well.

Place warm water and salt in a saucepan on high heat and bring to a boil. Add sea asparagus and blanch for 10 seconds. Drain in a colander and cool quickly under cold running water to stop the cook-ing and to retain the green colour.

Deep-fry sea cucumber strips in batches for 1 minute each. Drain on paper towels.

TO SERVE: Pour a small pool of warm vinaigrette on each warmed serving plate. Arrange sea asparagus on top of the vinaigrette, then top with sea cucumber. Garnish with basil.

Pan-roasted MUSSELS and Clams with Sizzling Brown Butter and Capers

. . . .

*T*HIS IS A VERY SIMPLE WAY to cook mussels and clams. You can also make this recipe with any other shellfish.

Makes 4 servings

Wash clams well. Wash mussels, making sure to remove and discard their beards.

Heat olive oil in two large cast-iron frying pans on high heat. Add clams and half the thyme to one of the pans and cook for 1 minute. Add mussels and the remaining thyme to the other frying pan and cook for 1 minute. Divide butter and capers between the two pans. Continue cooking clams and mussels for 2 to 3 minutes, until they open.

TO SERVE: Place clams and mussels and the butter in which they cooked in a warmed serving bowl and sprinkle with fleur de sel. Toast focaccia or garlic bread and serve on the side, to soak up the butter at the bottom of the bowl.

2 lbs/900 g Manila clams

2 lbs/900 g mussels

1 Tbsp/15 mL olive oil

¼ cup/60 mL chopped fresh thyme

1¼ cups/300 mL butter

2 Tbsp/30 mL capers

Fleur de sel

1 loaf focaccia or garlic bread, sliced

Pink Shell SCALLOPS, Manila Clams and
Mussels Sautéed in Lobster Oil

. . . .

WE HAVE LOTS of pink shell scallops around Vancouver Island. They are very tasty sautéed with mussels and clams. The meat is sweet and delicate, and they can simply be sautéed with garlic butter and then deglazed with white wine. Serve with wedges of lemon, garlic croutons or freshly baked cornbread.

Makes 4 servings

Wash clams well. Wash mussels, making sure to remove and discard their beards. Wash scallops.

Heat lobster oil in a frying pan on medium heat and sauté shallot for 2 minutes, until it becomes translucent. Add clams and a pinch of salt and pepper. Cover with a lid and cook for 1 minute. Turn up the heat to high. Add mussels and wine, cover with a lid and cook for 1 minute. Stir in whipping cream, parsley and tarragon. Add scallops. Cover with a lid and cook for 2 minutes, until shells open.

TO SERVE: Transfer contents of the frying pan to a heated serving bowl. Serve with wedges of lemon.

1 lb/450 g Manila clams

1 lb/450 g mussels

1 lb/450 g pink shell scallops

⅓ cup/75 mL lobster oil (page 166) or olive oil

1 shallot, chopped

1 cup/250 mL Sauvignon Blanc

½ cup/125 mL whipping cream

1 Tbsp/15 mL chopped fresh parsley

1 Tbsp/15 mL chopped fresh tarragon

1 lemon, quartered

Neon squid Saté-style
with Peanut Sauce

. . . .

SQUID

1 lb/450 g neon squid, cleaned,
  no tentacles

½ cup/125 mL soy sauce

2 cloves garlic, chopped

2 Tbsp/30 mL chopped fresh cilantro

2 tsp/10 mL liquid honey

1 tsp/5 mL chopped fresh ginger

SAUCE

⅓ cup/75 mL smooth unsweetened
  peanut butter

⅓ cup/75 mL rice vinegar

1 Tbsp/15 mL sesame oil

1 Tbsp/15 mL chopped fresh cilantro

1½ tsp/7.5 mL pickled ginger

¼ tsp/1 mL sambal oelek

¼ cup/60 mL water

SALAD

2 cups/250 mL mixed pea shoots
  and pea tips or micro greens

3 Tbsp/45 mL sesame oil

1 Tbsp/15 mL sesame seeds

SATÉ IS A COMMON SNACK all over Asia. This version uses neon squid, which is a local product that is very easy to cook on the barbecue or in a frying pan with a drop of oil. Don't overcook the squid, or it will turn rubbery. Chicken or any fish or shellfish will also work well in this recipe.

Pea tips are firmer than pea shoots, but you can use either.

Makes 4 servings

SQUID: Soak 24 bamboo skewers in water for 2 hours so that they will not burn on the barbecue.

Cut squid into strips 3 inches/7.5 cm long and ¾ inch/2 cm wide and place them in a bowl.

Place soy sauce, garlic, cilantro, honey and ginger in a blender or food processor. Mix for 20 seconds. Pour over squid. Cover and marinate in the refrigerator for 2 hours.

SAUCE: Place peanut butter, rice vinegar, sesame oil, cilantro, pickled ginger, sambal oelek and water in a blender or food processor and mix for 2 minutes. Cover and refrigerate until needed.

FINISH SQUID: Preheat the barbecue on medium heat. Thread marinated squid strips onto the bamboo skewers and grill on the barbecue for 2 minutes, until golden. Turn over and cook for 1 minute, until golden brown.

SALAD: Toss pea shoots and pea tips with sesame oil and sesame seeds in a bowl; season to taste with salt and pepper.

TO SERVE: Place squid skewers on a serving platter. Arrange salad beside the skewers and serve peanut sauce in a bowl on the side.

Sautéed COCKLES with
Chili, Garlic and Thai Basil

. . . .

COCKLES ARE A SHELLFISH that are not really known in North America, but you can sometimes find them at the market. This is the way I prepared them when I was working in Thailand, where they are very popular. Serve this dish with steamed rice, if you like, or double the recipe and serve it as a main course.

Makes 4 servings

Heat sesame oil in a wok or a large frying pan on medium heat. Sauté onion, ginger and chili pepper for 4 minutes, until golden. Stir in red Thai curry paste and cook for 1 minute. Turn up the heat to high and add cockles, fish stock, coconut milk, fish sauce and oyster sauce. Cover with a lid and cook for 3 minutes, until cockles open. Add basil and cilantro. Season to taste with salt and pepper, then stir in lime juice.

TO SERVE: Transfer contents to a warm serving bowl.

1 tsp/5 mL sesame oil

1 onion, sliced

1½ tsp/7.5 mL grated fresh ginger

1 chili pepper, chopped

1 tsp/5 mL red Thai curry paste

2 lbs/900 g cockles

½ cup/125 mL fish stock (page 162)

½ cup/125 mL coconut milk

1 Tbsp/15 mL fish sauce

1 Tbsp/15 mL oyster sauce

2 Tbsp/30 mL chopped fresh Thai basil

1 Tbsp/15 mL chopped fresh cilantro

1 lime, juice of

Pacific SALMON ROE with Wild Rice Galettes
and Lemon-Dill Crème Fraîche

. . . .

CRÈME FRAÎCHE

⅔ cup/150 mL whipping cream

2 tsp/10 mL buttermilk

1 lemon, juice of

⅓ cup/75 mL sour cream

4 tsp/20 mL chopped fresh dill

GALETTES

¾ cup/175 mL all-purpose flour

¼ cup/60 mL wild rice flour

2 tsp/10 mL baking powder

¼ tsp/1 mL salt

1 egg

1 cup/250 mL milk

1 Tbsp/15 mL liquid honey

2 Tbsp/30 mL butter, melted

1 Tbsp/15 mL chopped fresh chives

1 Tbsp/15 mL chopped fresh parsley

Drop of vegetable oil

4 oz/115 g preserved wild salmon roe

1 Tbsp/15 mL chopped chervil
  for garnish

1 Tbsp/15 mL chopped chives
  for garnish

½ lemon, zest of

*T*HIS REFRESHING APPETIZER makes a great party canapé or appetizer. A galette is a flat, flaky pancake. The wild rice flour gives this version an interesting flavour, but if you cannot find wild rice flour, substitute corn or whole wheat flour.

At The Cannery, we use sockeye roe, which we prefer to spring salmon roe because of its smaller size, nice colour and finer texture. However, either kind will give excellent results.

Makes 4 servings

CRÈME FRAÎCHE: Combine whipping cream and buttermilk in a bowl, cover and leave at room temperature for 30 hours. The cream will thicken.

Gently whisk in lemon juice, sour cream and dill. Season to taste with salt and pepper. Cover and refrigerate until needed.

GALETTES: Combine all-purpose flour, wild rice flour, baking powder and salt in a bowl. Make a well in the middle of the mixture and whisk in egg. Whisking very gently, slowly add milk, honey, melted butter, chives and parsley. The consistency should be like pancake batter.

Place a nonstick frying pan on medium-low heat, then add a drop of vegetable oil and spread it around with a pastry brush. Add 1 Tbsp/15 mL batter for each galette and cook two at a time for 2 minutes, until bubbles form on the top. Turn over and cook for 1 minute, until galettes puff up and become firm. Transfer to a heated serving platter. Repeat to make 8 galettes.

TO SERVE: Place a dollop of crème fraîche on each galette and top with salmon roe. Garnish with chervil, chives and lemon zest.

Giant SCALLOPS Marinated
in Ginger and Brown Sugar with Peanut
Vinaigrette and Pea Shoot Salad

. . . .

12 size U-10 scallops (page 3)

½ cup/125 mL brown sugar

2 Tbsp/30 mL fresh grated ginger

2 tsp/10 mL sambal oelek

2 Tbsp/30 mL sesame oil

2 cups/500 mL pea shoots (page 30)
  or bean sprouts

1 Tbsp/15 mL chopped fresh cilantro

½ cup/125 mL peanut vinaigrette
  (page 166)

*B*E CAREFUL not to overmarinate the scallops, otherwise you will dry them out. For variety, try this recipe with Ahi tuna or Pacific salmon.

Makes 4 servings

Remove and discard tendons of scallops (the small white firm piece attached to the flesh).

Place brown sugar, ginger and sambal oelek in a food processor and mix well until mixture becomes liquid. Transfer to a bowl and add scallops. Cover and marinate in the refrigerator for 3 hours.

Rinse scallops lightly under cold running water and dry on paper towels. Heat 1½ tsp/7.5 mL of the sesame oil in a nonstick frying pan on medium heat. Turn up the heat to high, then sear scallops for 2 minutes on each side, until light brown. Turn down the heat to low and cook for 2 minutes, until soft yet firm. Season to taste with salt and pepper.

Combine pea shoots, cilantro and the remaining sesame oil in a bowl. Toss together gently. Season to taste with salt and pepper.

TO SERVE: Place salad in the middle of 4 serving plates and arrange 3 scallops around the edge of each. Drizzle peanut vinaigrette around the scallops.

Baked Cherry TOMATOES,
Onion and Goat Cheese on Puff Pastry
with Tomato-Basil Sauce

. . . .

*T*HE SUCCESS OF THIS DISH depends on the tomatoes: be
sure they are fully ripe. This is also a great party recipe. You
can prepare all of the ingredients a day ahead, then assemble it just
before the event. If you're feeding a crowd, make bite-size versions
and serve them as finger food.

To vary the recipe, try Roma tomatoes in place of cherry tomatoes. Or serve the filling on pieces of focaccia bread instead of pastry.
Makes 4 servings

PASTRY: Preheat the oven to 400°F/200°C. Line a cookie sheet
with parchment paper.

On a board sprinkled lightly with flour, roll out puff pastry to a
thickness of ⅛ inch/3 mm. Cut the pastry into 4 disks, each 5 inches/
12.5 cm in diameter, and place them upside down on the prepared
cookie sheet. Use a pastry brush to gently brush off the excess flour.
Refrigerate until needed.

Heat olive oil and water in a nonstick frying pan on low heat.
Add onion and cook for 15 minutes, until golden. Add tomato paste,
thyme, and salt and pepper to taste, and cook for 1 minute.

Arrange onion and cherry tomatoes on the pastry disks and top
with goat cheese. Bake in the oven for 20 minutes, until the pastry
is cooked and puffy.

SAUCE: Heat a few drops of the olive oil in a frying pan on medium
heat. Sauté shallot and Roma tomatoes for 5 minutes, until soft. Add
balsamic vinegar and cook until reduced to half.

Transfer to a blender and mix for 1 minute while slowly adding
the remaining olive oil and chopped basil. Season to taste with salt
and pepper.

TO SERVE: Place the cooked tarts on a warmed serving plate. Garnish
with the basil leaves and serve with a bowl of warm sauce on the side.

PASTRY

12 oz/340 g frozen puff pastry,
 thawed
1 Tbsp/15 mL olive oil
¼ cup/60 mL water
1 onion, sliced
1 tsp/5 mL tomato paste
1 tsp/5 mL chopped fresh thyme
1 lb/450 g cherry tomatoes
4 oz/115 g soft goat cheese
4 leaves fresh basil for garnish

SAUCE

½ cup/125 mL olive oil
1 shallot, chopped
2 Roma tomatoes, chopped
1 Tbsp/15 mL balsamic vinegar
1 Tbsp/15 mL chopped fresh basil

Maple Syrup–glazed
Smoked SABLEFISH with Shallot Compote and
Frisée Lettuce with Hazelnut Vinaigrette

. . . .

*S*ABLEFISH, known as black cod or *morue charbonnière,* has an oily texture and a rich flavour. It can be found at the market naturally smoked and usually frozen at sea. If you cannot find smoked sablefish, you can use smoked haddock.

Makes 4 servings

SABLEFISH: Cut sablefish into 4 equal pieces and place in a bowl. Add ¼ cup/60 mL of the maple syrup and marinate for 4 hours in the refrigerator.

Preheat the oven to 375°F/190°C. Remove sablefish from marinade. Discard marinade. Place hazelnut oil in an ovenproof frying pan, add sablefish and bake in the oven for 10 to 12 minutes, until cooked. While fish is cooking, prepare the compote and salad.

COMPOTE: Melt butter in a saucepan on medium heat and sauté shallots and wine for 4 minutes, until reduced to one quarter. Add thyme and port, then reduce to half, about 3 minutes. Remove from the heat.

SALAD: In a bowl, combine Dijon mustard, red wine vinegar and salt and pepper to taste. Mix well, then slowly add the hazelnut oil. Place lettuce in a bowl and add vinaigrette. Toss gently, then season to taste with freshly ground black pepper.

TO SERVE: Divide salad among serving plates and sprinkle with chervil. Remove fish from the oven and place a piece on top of the salad on each serving. Place the frying pan in which you cooked the fish on low heat. Add the remaining maple syrup and cook for 4 minutes. Add sherry vinegar, deglaze the pan and cook until reduced to half. Remove sauce from the heat, then pour over the fish. Serve the shallot compote in a bowl on the side.

SABLEFISH

12 oz/340 g smoked sablefish
½ cup/125 mL maple syrup
1 tsp/5 mL hazelnut oil
¼ cup/60 mL sherry vinegar

COMPOTE

1 tsp/5 mL butter
1 cup/250 mL sliced shallots
½ cup/125 mL Shiraz
1 sprig fresh thyme
6 Tbsp/90 mL ruby port

SALAD

1½ tsp/7.5 mL Dijon mustard
1 Tbsp/15 mL red wine vinegar
3 Tbsp/45 mL hazelnut oil
8 oz/225 g frisée lettuce
   (about 4 cups/1 L)
2 Tbsp/30 mL fresh chervil
   for garnish

Butter CLAMS
with Mussel Vinaigrette and
Wild Mushroom Fricassée

. . . .

2 lbs/900 g butter clams

1 lb/450 g wild mushrooms
  (chanterelles, cèpes, lobster)

2 Tbsp/30 mL hazelnut oil

2 Tbsp/30 mL butter

2 shallots, chopped

1 Tbsp/15 mL chopped fresh parsley

1 Tbsp/15 mL chopped fresh chives

1 Tbsp/15 mL cognac

¼ cup/125 mL creamy mussel
  vinaigrette (page 166)

8 sprigs fresh chervil for garnish

*B*UTTER CLAMS are very popular with First Nations peoples, and digging up these molluscs will keep kids busy at the beach. These clams have a very fragile shell, so when you collect them, be gentle, or you will find broken shells with the meat.

Makes 4 servings

Wash clams well.

Cut mushrooms into quarters or halves, depending on their size. Heat 1 Tbsp/15 mL of the hazelnut oil in a frying pan on medium heat. Sauté mushrooms for 8 minutes, until all the liquid is released. Remove from the heat and drain mushrooms in a colander. Reserve cooking liquid to make soup or stock.

In the same frying pan on low heat, melt 1 Tbsp/15 mL of the butter. Add half of the shallots and sauté for 1 minute. Add sautéed mushrooms, then turn up the heat to medium. Stir in parsley and chives, sauté briefly, then remove from the heat. Season to taste with salt and pepper. Keep warm.

In a clean frying pan on medium heat, heat the remaining hazelnut oil and butter. Sauté the remaining shallots for 1 minute. Turn up the heat to high, add clams and cook covered for 2 minutes, until the shells open. Add cognac, then step back from the stove and carefully light the cognac.

Let the flame die down, then use a slotted spoon to transfer clams to a heated serving platter. Continue cooking the liquid in the pan until reduced to half, then stir in mussel vinaigrette.

TO SERVE: Place mushrooms on a serving platter with clams. Pour the reduced liquid over clams and mushrooms. Garnish with chervil.

Pan-fried Panko-coated
RAZOR CLAMS with Smoked Herring
and Toasted Pecan Coleslaw

. . . .

*R*AZOR CLAMS are fun to dig for and also very fragile. To remove the sand, place them in a bowl under running water and leave them for an hour. Transfer the clams to paper towels and pat them dry. You can also use scallops or any fish fillet in this recipe. Similarly, you can make the coleslaw with any ingredients you wish.

Panko is a type of Japanese bread crumb that gives a really nice crispy texture to breaded food. It is sold in Asian and specialty food stores.

Makes 4 servings

COLESLAW: Place cabbage, red onion, carrot and herring in a bowl and toss together gently. Cover and refrigerate while you prepare the dressing.

Preheat the oven to 375°F/190°C. Place pecans on a cookie sheet and toast in the oven for 3 minutes. Stir gently and toast for 3 minutes. Remove from the oven, transfer to a plate and allow to cool. Chop roughly.

To make the dressing, combine pecans with parsley, ginger, lemon zest, lemon juice and mayonnaise in another bowl. Mix well and season to taste with salt and pepper. Cover and refrigerate for 30 minutes. Toss the coleslaw with the dressing. Cover the salad with plastic wrap and refrigerate until needed.

CLAMS: Combine egg, water, and salt and pepper to taste in a bowl. Place flour and panko on separate plates. Coat clams one by one with flour, dip into egg mixture (making sure clams are completely covered), then roll in panko to coat evenly.

Heat olive oil in a frying pan on medium heat and fry breaded clams for 1 minute. Turn clams over, add butter and cook for 1 minute, until golden. Drain on paper towels.

TO SERVE: Divide coleslaw among 4 serving plates. Arrange the clams beside the coleslaw, and garnish each plate with a sprig of parsley.

COLESLAW
⅓ green cabbage, thinly sliced
½ red onion, thinly sliced
1 carrot, julienned
2 fillets smoked herring, thinly sliced
3 Tbsp/45 mL pecans
1 Tbsp/15 mL chopped fresh parsley
1 tsp/5 mL chopped fresh ginger
1 lemon, zest and juice of
1 cup/250 mL mayonnaise

CLAMS
1 egg
2 Tbsp/30 mL water
2 Tbsp/30 mL all-purpose flour
1 cup/250 mL panko
   (Japanese bread crumbs)
12 oz/340 g razor clam meat
1 Tbsp/15 mL olive oil
2 Tbsp/30 mL butter
4 sprigs fresh Italian parsley
   for garnish

Pacific SARDINE Tempura with
Fennel Salad and Tapenade of Black Olives
and Sun-dried Tomatoes

. . . .

TAPENADE

3 sun-dried tomatoes

2 fillets anchovy

1 shallot

½ cup/125 mL niçoise olives, pitted

1 Tbsp/15 mL minced fresh Italian
   flat-leaf parsley

⅔ cup/150 mL extra-virgin olive oil

1 clove garlic

SALAD

2 Roma tomatoes

2 bulbs fennel

1 lemon, juice of

¼ cup/60 mL extra-virgin olive oil

SARDINE TEMPURA

8 cups/2 L canola or peanut oil for
   deep frying

½ cup/125 mL rice flour or all-
   purpose flour

½ cup/125 mL cornstarch

¾ cup/175 mL ice water

1 tsp/5 mL chopped fresh basil

4 whole sardines, each 8 oz/225 g,
   cut in half but joined at the tail
   (bone removed with tweezers)

4 leaves fresh basil

2 ice cubes

*P*EOPLE THINK OF SARDINES as a canned food. However, you can find fresh Pacific sardines at the market. Some people do not like sardines because they are bonier than other fish, but they have a rich flavour that's worth enjoying.

Sardines are a versatile fish. You can grill them on the barbecue and serve them with basil-shallot butter. Or, if you dislike the bones, you can marinate the sardines (marinating softens the bones) in coconut milk and lime as you would for a carpaccio.

Makes 4 servings

TAPENADE: Place sun-dried tomatoes in a bowl of cold water to soak overnight at room temperature. Drain the tomatoes and discard the soaking water.

Place drained tomatoes, anchovies, shallot, olives and parsley in a food processor. Mix well for 2 minutes while slowly adding olive oil and garlic until the mixture becomes a paste. Do not overmix. Cover and refrigerate until needed.

SALAD: Boil a pot of water on high heat. Add tomatoes and blanch for 5 to 10 seconds. Use a slotted spoon to transfer tomatoes to a bowl of iced water to cool down and stop the cooking. Use a knife to peel off the skin. Cut flesh into ¼-inch/5-mm dice.

Peel fennel bulbs and cut them in half. Remove and discard the hard part in the centre. Use a Japanese mandoline to slice fennel very thinly.

Place tomatoes, fennel, lemon juice and olive oil in a bowl and toss together gently. Season to taste with salt and pepper.

SARDINE TEMPURA: Preheat oil in the deep fryer to 375°F/190°C.

Combine flour and cornstarch in a bowl. Whisking all the while, slowly add water and chopped basil until batter is smooth.

Place a sardine on a plate and put a basil leaf between the fillets. Push a toothpick through the fish to keep it together. Repeat process for the rest of the sardines and basil.

Add two ice cubes to the tempura batter. Dip sardines into the batter one by one and deep-fry them, two at a time, for about 2 minutes. Drain on paper towels.

TO SERVE: Divide the salad among 4 plates and top each serving with a sardine tempura. Place 1 Tbsp/15 mL or more of the tapenade on the side of each serving. Extra tapenade can be refrigerated overnight and used on a sandwich or as a garnish for grilled fish.

Crispy SMELT

. . . .

CHILI MAYONNAISE

2 egg yolks

1½ tsp/7.5 mL Dijon mustard

¾ cup/175 mL vegetable oil

½ lemon, juice of

¼ tsp/1 mL sambal oelek

SMELT

8 cups/2 L canola oil or
    peanut oil for deep-frying

1½ lemons

2 lbs/900 g small smelt, 3 inches/
    7.5 cm long

½ cup/125 mL all-purpose flour

½ cup/125 mL cornmeal

⅓ cup/75 mL cornstarch

1½ cups/375 mL cold water

8 sprigs fresh parsley

1 tsp/5 mL fleur de sel

SMELT ARE AVAILABLE between January and April. They are rich in oil and can taste or smell like cucumber. They are very popular with First Nations peoples and can also be found in Europe, Eastern Europe and North America. To deep-fry the smelts, I like to use tempura batter, but you can simply use flour.

I prefer the very small smelt full of roe (look for a big, firm belly). The small ones cook quickly so the flesh stays crispy and the roe won't overcook.

Makes 4 servings

CHILI MAYONNAISE: In a food processor, mix egg yolks and Dijon mustard until well combined. Season with salt and pepper. With the motor running, slowly add vegetable oil, until the mixture becomes thick. Add lemon juice and sambal oelek. Cover with plastic wrap and refrigerate until needed.

SMELT: Preheat the oil in a deep fryer to 350°F/180°C.

Cut the whole lemon into 6 wedges.

Rinse smelt and drain on paper towels.

Mix together flour, cornmeal, cornstarch and water in a bowl. Add smelt and coat evenly with the batter. Take a handful of smelt at a time and deep-fry them for 2 minutes, then, using a slotted spoon, transfer them to a warmed plate. (The smelt should only be three quarters cooked.)

Deep-fry parsley sprigs and drain on paper towels.

To finish smelt, put them back into the deep fryer for 3 minutes, until they turn golden. Use a slotted spoon to remove fish, then drain on paper towels. Squeeze the half lemon over smelt and sprinkle with fleur de sel.

TO SERVE: Arrange smelt on a warmed platter. Garnish with lemon wedges and deep-fried parsley. Serve chili mayonnaise in a bowl on the side.

Spawn-on-Kelp TEMPURA with
Soy-Ginger Sauce and Daikon Salad

. . . .

*T*HE JAPANESE CONSIDER SPAWN (herring roe) on kelp to be a great delicacy. So do First Nations peoples on the Pacific Coast—they have been harvesting it from the sea for many generations. Most spawn on kelp is preserved in brine, so it is important to rinse it in a bowl under gently running water for an hour before making the recipe. Be sure to dry the roe on paper towels before deep-frying.

I like the contrast of tempura with the crunchiness of the roe over the kelp. The daikon salad gives the dish a fresh taste, and it is well balanced with the soy sauce.

Makes 4 servings

SAUCE: Heat sesame oil in a saucepan on low heat. Sauté ginger and shallot for 2 minutes, until shallot becomes translucent. Stir in soy sauce, sake and honey. Turn up the heat to high and bring to a boil, then turn down the heat to low.

In a cup, mix together water and cornstarch, then pour slowly into the boiling soy sauce mixture, whisking constantly, and cook for 2 minutes. Strain sauce through a sieve and allow to cool. Add grated daikon. Cover and refrigerate until needed.

SALAD: Peel and finely grate daikon into a bowl. Add pickled ginger, sugar, rice vinegar and sesame oil. Toss gently. Season to taste with salt and pepper. Cover and refrigerate for about 1 hour.

TEMPURA: Heat oil in the deep fryer to 350°F/180°C. Cut spawn on kelp into strips 3 inches/6 cm long × ½ inch/1 cm.

To make tempura batter, combine rice flour, cornstarch, sesame seeds and a pinch of salt in a bowl. While whisking, slowly add ice water.

Add two ice cubes to the tempura batter. Dip spawn on kelp strips one at a time into the tempura batter, coat well and then quickly place them all, one by one, into the deep fryer. Shake the fryer basket so that the strips do not stick to each other or to the basket. Cook for about 1 minute, until crispy. Drain on paper towels.

TO SERVE: Stir daikon salad with a spoon, then remove and discard the excess liquid. Place daikon salad on a serving platter, add tempura and serve sauce in a separate bowl on the side.

SAUCE

1 tsp/5 mL sesame oil

1 tsp/5 mL grated fresh ginger

1 Tbsp/15 mL chopped shallot

½ cup/125 mL light soy sauce

⅛ cup/30 mL sake

1½ tsp/7.5 mL honey

1½ tsp/7.5 mL water

1½ tsp/7.5 mL cornstarch

1 tsp/5 mL grated daikon

SALAD

1 cup/250 mL daikon

1 Tbsp/15 mL chopped pickled ginger

½ tsp/2.5 mL sugar

1 Tbsp/15 mL rice vinegar

1 Tbsp/15 mL sesame oil

TEMPURA

8 cups/2 L oil (vegetable, canola, peanut) for deep-frying

11 oz/300 g spawn on kelp

½ cup/125 mL rice flour

¼ cup/60 mL cornstarch

1 tsp/5 mL toasted sesame seeds

½ cup/125 mL ice water

2 ice cubes

Wild MUSHROOMS
Sautéed with Port Demi-glace

. . . .

DEMI-GLACE

1 Tbsp/15 mL butter

2 shallots, sliced

1 sprig fresh thyme, chopped

½ tsp/2.5 mL freshly cracked
    black pepper

¼ cup/60 mL ruby port

1½ cups/375 mL vegetable stock
    (page 163)

1 cup/250 mL soy milk

2 Tbsp/30 mL hazelnut oil

MUSHROOMS

7 oz/200 g chanterelles, about
    8½ cups/625 mL

7 oz/200 g cèpes (porcini), about
    8½ cups/625 mL

7 oz/200 g lobster mushrooms,
    about 8½ cups/625 mL

A few drops of hazelnut oil

1 tsp/5 mL unsalted butter

2 shallots, chopped

1 tsp/5 mL chopped garlic

1 Tbsp/15 mL chopped fresh chives

1 Tbsp/15 mL chopped fresh parsley

4 breadsticks for garnish

4 sprigs fresh chervil for garnish

*I*N CANADA WE HAVE a large variety of wild mushrooms. The spring brings morels, followed by chanterelles, cauliflower mushrooms, yellow-foot chanterelles, lobster mushrooms and cèpes. I like to pair hazelnut oil with the wild mushrooms, but you can also use regular vegetable oil or butter. Serve the mushrooms with or without the sauce on the side.

Makes 4 servings

DEMI-GLACE: Melt 1 tsp/5 mL of the butter in a saucepan on medium heat. Sauté shallots, thyme and black pepper for 5 minutes, until shallots are golden. Stir in port and cook until reduced to one quarter, about 1 minute. Add stock and soy milk and cook on high heat until reduced to half, about 14 minutes.

Transfer the sauce to a blender and mix for 1 minute on high speed while slowly pouring in hazelnut oil. Strain demi-glace through a sieve into a clean saucepan.

MUSHROOMS: Trim and discard stems of chanterelles, cèpes and lobster mushrooms. Fill the sink with cold water and wash the mushrooms well, then drain in a colander. Repeat this process two more times. Cut the mushrooms into halves or quarters so that the pieces are roughly the same size. Drain on paper towels.

Heat hazelnut oil in a nonstick frying pan on high heat. Sauté chanterelles for 3 minutes, until they are soft and release their juices. Add salt and pepper and drain in a colander. Save the juice and mushrooms separately. Repeat the process for cèpes and lobster mushrooms. Pour the combined mushroom jus into the demi-glace and cook on low heat for 5 minutes.

Melt butter in a clean saucepan on medium heat and sauté shallots for 2 minutes, until translucent. Add garlic and turn up the heat to high. Add chanterelles, cèpes and lobster mushrooms, then sauté for 2 minutes, until warmed. Season to taste with salt and pepper. Stir in chives and parsley.

TO SERVE: Place the saucepan of demi-glace on medium heat, add the remaining butter and cook for 1 minute. Season to taste with salt and pepper.

Place 2 Tbsp/30 mL of the demi-glace at the bottom of 4 warmed deep serving plates, and top with mushrooms. Garnish each serving with a breadstick and a sprig of chervil. Serve the remaining demi-glace in a sauceboat on the side.

Dungeness Crab Cakes with
Nori Mayonnaise and Jicama Salad

. . . .

*T*HESE CAKES are great made with crab, but you can also use salmon, prawns, shrimp or corn. Preparing the crab mixture the day before will make it easier to work with. You can also double the quantities and keep the cakes premade (tightly wrapped in plastic wrap) in the freezer for up to 10 days. When needed, simply thaw the cakes overnight in the refrigerator. For a quick meal, serve them with mixed greens rather than the jicama salad.

Jicama, or "Mexican potato," is grown in Mexico, South America and Texas. It is tasty shredded and tossed with pickled ginger and sesame oil. Also, it stays crispy and sweet even when cooked.

Makes 4 servings

NORI MAYONNAISE: Combine rice vinegar and a pinch of salt in a bowl. Roughly chop the nori, then place it in the vinegar mixture to soak for 15 minutes.

In another bowl, mix together egg yolks and Dijon mustard. Add salt and pepper to taste. Whisking constantly, slowly add oil until the mixture becomes thick. Still whisking constantly, add softened nori, lemon juice and pickled ginger. Refrigerate until needed.

CRAB CAKES: Place fish in a food processor and mix for 2 minutes. Add egg white and mix for 20 seconds. With the motor running, slowly add whipping cream until mixture is smooth and silky.

In a bowl, combine mayonnaise, crabmeat, cilantro, parsley, red onion and green onion. Add fish mixture and mix well. Season to taste with salt and pepper. Cover and refrigerate for 1 hour.

Divide crab mixture into 8 equal portions. Using your hands, make 8 patties, 3 inches/7.5 cm in diameter and ½ inch/1 cm thick. Roll the crab cakes in panko, making sure they are well coated.

Heat olive oil in a nonstick frying pan on medium heat. Sauté crab cakes for 3 minutes. Turn over and cook for 4 minutes, until golden. Drain on paper towels.

SALAD: Place jicama in a bowl with rice vinegar, sesame oil and sesame seeds, and toss gently. Season to taste with salt and pepper.

TO SERVE: Place two crab cakes on each plate. Arrange salad beside the crab cakes. Serve nori mayonnaise in a bowl on the side.

NORI MAYONNAISE

1 Tbsp/15 mL rice vinegar

½ sheet nori (the kind used for sushi)

8 egg yolks

1½ tsp/7.5 mL Dijon mustard

¾ cup/175 mL vegetable oil

½ tsp/2.5 mL lemon juice

1 Tbsp/15 mL pickled ginger

CRAB CAKES

4 oz/115 g fish (snapper,
    halibut, salmon)

½ egg white

½ cup/125 mL whipping cream

½ cup/125 mL mayonnaise

8 oz/225 g fresh Dungeness
    crabmeat

1 Tbsp/15 mL chopped fresh cilantro

1 Tbsp/15 mL chopped fresh parsley

½ red onion, chopped

1 green onion, chopped

1 cup/250 mL panko (Japanese
    bread crumbs) (page 39)

1 tsp/5 mL olive oil

SALAD

1 lb/450 g jicama, julienned

¼ cup/60 mL rice vinegar

1 Tbsp/15 mL sesame oil

1 Tbsp/15 mL toasted sesame seeds

Warm DUCK Liver Parfait
with Belgian Endives and Walnuts

. . . .

PARFAIT

3½ oz/90 g duck liver

½ cup/125 mL milk

½ cup/125 mL butter

1 shallot, chopped

¼ cup/60 mL ruby port

1 cup/250 mL brown chicken
   stock (page 164)

2 eggs

½ tsp/2.5 mL liquid honey

3 Tbsp/45 mL whipping cream

4 sprigs fresh tarragon for garnish

ENDIVES AND WALNUTS

3 Belgian endives

1 Tbsp/15 mL butter

½ lemon, juice of

1 tsp/5 mL sugar

2 Tbsp/30 mL water

¼ cup/60 mL white vermouth

1 cup/250 mL whipping cream

1 Tbsp/15 mL cognac

½ tsp/2.5 mL chopped tarragon

3 Tbsp/45 mL chopped toasted
   walnuts

A VERY SIMPLE WAY to prepare duck liver, this recipe for duck parfait is very versatile. Make it a day ahead and serve it cold, spread on toasted bread. For a party, double the quantity and cook it in a terrine.

This parfait will keep in the refrigerator for 3 days. Note that if you cut a piece, the terrine will turn brown in 1 hour as the liver oxidizes with exposure to air. This may not look attractive, but it is an entirely natural process and does not affect the flavour.

Makes 4 servings

PARFAIT: Place duck liver and milk in a bowl, cover and allow to marinate in the refrigerator for 2 hours. This will remove any bitterness from the liver.

Preheat the oven to 350°F/180°C. Melt 1 tsp/5 mL of the butter and brush the insides of 4 ramekins with it.

Make a demi-glace by melting 1 tsp/5 mL of the butter in a saucepan on medium heat. Sauté shallot for 2 minutes, until translucent. Add port and cook until reduced to half, about 1 minute. Add stock and cook until reduced to one quarter, about 5 minutes. Strain demi-glace through a sieve into a clean bowl.

Melt the remaining butter in a clean saucepan on medium heat until golden brown.

Remove duck liver from milk and discard milk. Place liver, eggs and demi-glace in a blender and mix for 1 minute. With the motor running, slowly pour in melted butter, honey and whipping cream. Season to taste with salt and pepper. Pour into the prepared ramekins and cover the surface of each with plastic wrap.

Place the ramekins in a roasting pan and add hot water to reach halfway up the sides of the ramekins. Bake in the oven for 25 minutes, until set. Remove from the oven and allow to cool for 5 minutes.

ENDIVES AND WALNUTS: While ramekins are in the oven, prepare endives and walnuts.

Cut endives in half, then remove and discard the hard core. Remove the leaves and save. Combine 1 tsp/5 mL of the butter, lemon juice, sugar and water in a nonstick frying pan on medium heat. Add endive leaves, cover the pan with a lid and cook for 1 minute, until soft and translucent. Transfer endive leaves to a plate. To deglaze the frying pan, add vermouth and cook until reduced to half, about 5 minutes. Add whipping cream and cook until reduced to half. Stir the remaining butter into the sauce.

Transfer the sauce to a blender, season to taste with salt and pepper, add cognac and tarragon and mix well.

TO SERVE: Run a knife around the inside edge of the ramekins. Turn each one upside down on a separate serving plate.

Place endive leaves and sauce in a saucepan on low heat and cook for 1 minute to reheat. Stir in walnuts.

Remove endive leaves from the sauce, arrange some around each liver parfait, and garnish with a sprig of tarragon. Drizzle some sauce on the plate before serving.

SOUPS

. . . .

*T*HESE SOUPS

are very simple and easy to make at home.

The "exotic" ingredients can be found at most

public markets and Asian food stores.

Instead of using cream in the soup recipes, you

can use soy milk or low-fat sour cream.

I personally like to process my creamy soups in

a blender. This gives them a nice velvety

finish and a smooth texture.

Creamy MUSSEL and
Saffron Soup

. . . .

1½ lbs/680 g mussels

1 Tbsp/15 mL olive oil

1 shallot, sliced

Pinch of saffron

2 Tbsp/30 mL butter

¼ cup/60 mL all-purpose flour

1 bouquet garni (page 15)

1 cup/250 mL Sauvignon Blanc

2½ cups/625 mL fish stock
   (page 162)

1 cup/250 mL whipping cream

1 Tbsp/15 mL chopped fresh
   chervil for garnish

*M*USSELS AND SAFFRON go very well together. I like to use local mussels, especially the sweet, flavourful ones from Saltspring Island. Always use real saffron. Although it is expensive, you don't need very much of it. Look for a pistil that is deep red and doesn't break when you touch it.

Makes 4 servings

Wash mussels, making sure to remove and discard their beards.

Heat olive oil in a stockpot on medium heat. Sauté shallot and saffron for 2 minutes, until shallot becomes translucent. Stir in butter and flour, then cook for 1 minute. Add mussels and bouquet garni, then cook for 1 minute. Add wine, cover pot with a lid and cook for 5 minutes, or until mussels open.

Use a slotted spoon to remove mussels. Take out meat and set aside for garnish, discarding the shells. Leave the stock in the pot.

Add fish stock and whipping cream to the stockpot. Whisk well and cook for 10 minutes. Strain through a sieve and discard solids and bouquet garni. Allow soup to cool slightly, then place it in a blender and mix briefly. Season to taste with salt and pepper.

TO SERVE: Pour soup into a tureen. Garnish with the reserved mussel meat and sprinkle with chervil.

FISH Soup, Mediterranean-style

. . . .

*T*HIS IS A TRADITIONAL Mediterranean-style soup, which is full of flavour. Use any combination of fish you like, as long as they are saltwater fish; the freshwater varieties do not have enough flavour for this dish.

Rouille is a rust-coloured sauce made from red bell peppers, garlic and saffron, and finished with olive oil. It is a staple of Provençal cuisine, where it is used mainly as a garnish for fish soups and stews such as bouillabaisse. Make the rouille and the croutons one day ahead, if you want to save time.

Makes 4 servings

CROUTONS: Cut baguette at an angle into 8 slices, each ¼ inch/ 5 mm thick. Heat olive oil in a large frying pan on medium heat and pan-fry baguette slices until golden brown. Turn over and toast the other side. Drain on paper towels. Rub garlic over both sides of each toasted baguette slice.

ROUILLE: Place potato in a saucepan, add enough cold water to cover and stir in a pinch of rock salt. Bring to a boil on medium heat and cook for 15 minutes, until fork-tender. Drain and place in a food processor. Add red bell pepper, garlic and saffron. Purée until smooth. With the motor running, slowly add olive oil. Season to taste with salt and pepper.

SOUP: Heat olive oil in a stockpot on medium heat. Sauté fennel, onion, leek, celery, tomato and garlic for 10 minutes, until they become soft and translucent. Stir in tomato paste and saffron, then cook for 2 minutes. Turn down the heat to low. Add fish bones and salmon heads, stir mixture well, and cook for 5 minutes. Add wine and cook for 1 minute. Add fish stock and thyme, then turn up the heat to medium and cook for 20 minutes.

Use a hand-held blender to purée soup until smooth. Strain through a sieve into a clean saucepan on medium heat and bring to a boil. Cook for 2 minutes, then remove and discard the fat and foam from the top. Add basil. Season to taste with salt and pepper.

TO SERVE: Pour soup into a tureen. Serve garlic croutons and rouille in separate bowls on the side.

CROUTONS
1 French baguette

⅓ cup/75 mL olive oil

4 cloves garlic, halved and centre germs removed

ROUILLE
1 Yukon Gold potato, peeled, in 1-inch/2.5-cm cubes

Pinch of rock salt

¼ red bell pepper, deseeded and roughly chopped

3 cloves garlic, halved

Pinch of saffron

⅓ cup/75 mL olive oil

SOUP
1 tsp/5 mL extra-virgin olive oil

½ bulb fennel, thinly sliced

1 onion, thinly sliced

½ leek, white part only, thinly sliced

1 stalk celery, thinly sliced

1 tomato, thinly sliced

3 cloves garlic, chopped

1 Tbsp/15 mL tomato paste

Pinch of saffron

8 oz/225 g fish bones (snapper, perch, rock cod)

8 oz/225 g salmon heads, in 1-inch/2.5-cm cubes

½ cup/125 mL Sauvignon Blanc

8 cups/2 L fish stock (page 162)

1 sprig fresh thyme, chopped

2 Tbsp/30 mL chopped fresh basil

CLAM Chowder

. . . .

1 lb/450 g clams

1 Tbsp/15 mL olive oil

2 shallots, in ¼-inch/½-cm cubes

1 tsp/5 mL chopped garlic

½ cup/125 mL Sauvignon Blanc

1 bouquet garni (page 15)

½ onion, in ¼-inch/½-cm cubes

½ bulb fennel, in ¼-inch/½-cm cubes

½ leek, in ¼-inch/½-cm cubes

1 stalk celery, in ¼-inch/½-cm cubes

2 Tbsp/30 mL butter

1 Tbsp + 2 tsp/25 mL all-purpose
   flour

2½ cups/625 mL fish stock
   (page 162)

8 oz/225 g yellow-fleshed potatoes,
   in ¼-inch/½-cm cubes

1 cup/250 mL whipping cream

1 Tbsp/15 mL chopped fresh parsley
   for garnish (optional)

CLAM CHOWDER IS RICH in flavour and can be a full meal on its own, served with a nice crusty bread. To vary it, you can add smoked salmon or mussels, or a bit of jalapeño pepper or fresh corn kernels. It is all up to your imagination.

Makes 4 servings

Wash clams well.

Heat half of the olive oil in a saucepan on medium heat. Sauté shallots and garlic for 2 minutes, or until they become translucent. Add clams, wine and bouquet garni. Cover the pot with a lid and cook for 4 minutes, or until clams open.

Use a slotted spoon to remove clams and bouquet garni. Discard bouquet garni. Take out meat from clams. Save meat and clam juice but discard the shells.

Heat the remaining olive oil in another saucepan on medium heat. Sauté onion, fennel, leek and celery for 2 minutes, or until they become translucent. Add butter and flour, then mix well. Whisk in the reserved clam juice and fish stock. Add salt to taste and cook for 5 minutes. Add potatoes and cook for 15 minutes. Add whipping cream and clam meat, then cook for 5 minutes.

TO SERVE: Divide among warmed soup bowls and garnish with parsley.

Creamy Beach
OYSTER Soup

. . . .

12 large beach oysters

3 Tbsp/45 mL butter

½ bulb fennel, sliced

3 shallots, sliced

1 leek, white part only, sliced

3 Tbsp/45 mL all-purpose flour

4 cups/1 L fish stock (page 162)

1 bouquet garni (page 15)

1 cup/250 mL whipping cream

1 Tbsp/15 mL chopped fresh
    chervil for garnish

1 Tbsp/15 mL chopped fresh
    chives for garnish

*T*HIS IS ONE of my favourite soups. I like the taste of oysters in a soup and I love the contrast of cream and oysters. In this soup, I like to use large beach oysters from Harmony Bay on the Sunshine Coast because their juice gives it a delicate taste.

Makes 4 servings

Shuck oysters (page 3) and remove meat, saving the meat and juices. Discard the shells.

Melt 1 Tbsp/15 mL of the butter in a saucepan on medium heat and sauté fennel, shallots and leek for 2 minutes, until shallots are translucent. Add the remaining butter and flour, mixing well, and cook for 1 minute. Add 10 of the oysters with their reserved juices and sauté for 1 minute. Slowly add stock while whisking gently to get rid of lumps. Add bouquet garni and cook for 8 minutes. Stir in whipping cream and cook for 3 minutes. Use a slotted spoon to remove and discard bouquet garni.

Add the remaining 2 oysters and purée the soup, using a hand-held blender, until smooth, about 2 minutes. Strain through a sieve into a clean tureen. Season to taste with salt and pepper.

TO SERVE: Garnish the soup with chervil and chives.

South Asian
SALMON Soup
. . . .

THIS IS A CLASSIC Thai soup with a twist. The smoked salmon gives it a rich smoky flavour. This recipe makes a mild-tasting soup, so if you like it spicier, just increase the chili a little bit.
Makes 4 servings

Heat sesame oil in a saucepan on medium heat and sauté onion for 2 minutes, until translucent. Stir in chili paste and cook for 30 seconds, then add fish stock. Add salmon head and cook for 35 minutes. Add lime juice, fish sauce, lemon grass, galangal and mushrooms, then cook for 5 minutes. Add diced salmon and cook for 1 minute. Remove and discard salmon head. Season to taste with salt and pepper.

TO SERVE: Add smoked salmon, chili pepper, garlic, Thai basil, cilantro and kaffir lime leaves to soup. Pour into warmed soup bowls.

1 Tbsp/15 mL sesame oil

1 onion, sliced

½ tsp/2.5 mL red chili paste
    (for a mild flavour)

4 cups/1 L fish stock (page 162)

1 salmon head, wrapped in
    cheesecloth

3 limes, juice of

1 Tbsp/15 mL Thai fish sauce

½ stalk lemon grass, sliced

1 Tbsp/15 mL galangal, sliced

4 oz/115 g mushrooms, quartered
    (wild if in season, such as
    chanterelles, cèpes, etc.)

4 oz/115 g salmon, in ½-inch/
    1-cm cubes

1½ oz/45 g smoked salmon,
    julienned

1 chili pepper, cut in half,
    half the seeds removed and
    flesh finely minced

1 clove garlic, chopped

1 Tbsp/15 mL chopped fresh
    Thai basil

1 Tbsp/15 mL chopped fresh cilantro

3 kaffir lime leaves, julienned

Roma TOMATO, Basil and
Black Bean Soup

. . . .

PESTO

1 Tbsp/15 mL fresh parsley leaves

1 Tbsp/15 mL fresh basil leaves

6 Tbsp/90 mL extra-virgin olive oil

1 Tbsp/15 mL garlic

1 Tbsp/15 mL pine nuts

SOUP

⅔ cup/160 mL dried black beans

3 cups/750 mL cold water

1 Tbsp/15 mL olive oil

½ red onion, chopped

½ tsp/2.5 mL anise seeds

1 tsp/5 mL chopped garlic

1 Tbsp/15 mL tomato paste

8 cups/2 L vegetable stock
   (page 163)

1 lb/450 g Roma tomatoes, in
   ½-inch/1-cm cubes

1 cup/250 mL fresh basil leaves

2 Tbsp/30 mL freshly grated
   Parmesan cheese

1 lime, juice of

*T*HIS RUSTIC SOUP is full of flavour and chunky vegetables, and it is made even tastier with a splash of lime juice at the end. You can make this soup with any beans you like (navy, red, lima), and you can save time by soaking the beans a day ahead. Serve with a slice of toasted or grilled cornbread.

Makes 4 servings

PESTO: Place parsley, basil and olive oil in a blender and mix for 2 minutes. Add garlic and mix for 20 seconds. Add pine nuts and mix for 30 seconds. Cover and refrigerate (will keep for up to 4 days).

SOUP: Place black beans and water in a bowl and let soak overnight at room temperature.

Heat olive oil in a saucepan on medium heat. Sauté red onion, anise seeds and garlic for 5 minutes, until light golden. Stir in tomato paste and cook for 1 minute. Drain beans, add to the saucepan and cook for 1 minute. Add stock and tomatoes, then cook for 35 minutes, until beans are soft. Add basil. Remove from the heat and season to taste with salt and pepper.

TO SERVE: Pour soup into warm serving bowls and garnish each with 1 tsp/5 mL of the pesto, Parmesan cheese and lime juice.

Creamy Green LENTIL
and Smoked Bacon Soup

. . . .

I USE PUY (French green) lentils in this soup because I like their earthy flavour and texture. However, you can try different kinds of lentils. Look in Indian food markets, which usually offer an interesting variety. Bacon also gives this soup a rich yet rustic flavour.

Makes 4 servings

Place lentils and water in a bowl and let soak overnight at room temperature.

Melt butter in a saucepan on medium heat. Sauté onion and leek for 2 minutes, until soft and translucent. Add bacon slab and bay leaf, then cook for 2 minutes. Turn bacon slab over.

Drain soaked lentils and discard water. Rinse lentils in a sieve under cold running water. Place lentils in the saucepan with sautéed vegetables and bacon. Add stock and simmer for 30 minutes.

Remove bacon and set aside. Remove and discard bay leaf. Stir in whipping cream and cook for 5 minutes, then remove soup from the heat and allow to cool. Transfer to a blender and purée until smooth.

Cut the cooked bacon into ¼-inch/5-mm cubes. Remove and discard large stems from parsley, then chop roughly.

TO SERVE: Reheat soup and pour into a tureen. Garnish with bacon and parsley.

8 oz/225 g Puy lentils

4 cups/1 L water

1 Tbsp/15 mL unsalted butter

½ onion, chopped

½ leek, white part only, sliced

4 oz/115 g bacon, in one piece

1 bay leaf

3 cups/750 mL vegetable stock
  (page 163)

½ cup/125 mL whipping cream

½ bunch fresh Italian flat-leaf parsley

Chilled CUCUMBER and Dill Soup
with Preserved Salmon Roe

. . . .

*T*HIS IS A VERY REFRESHING summer soup that you can prepare in just 5 minutes, which makes it perfect if you have last-minute visitors. I like to use sockeye salmon roe because of its smaller size, which looks and tastes more delicate. If you cannot find preserved salmon roe, regular salmon roe is fine.

Makes 4 servings

Peel and cut cucumbers in half lengthwise, then remove and discard seeds. Cut cucumbers into rough chunks. Peel garlic and cut in half; remove and discard the centre germ.

Place cucumber and garlic in a blender. Add milk and purée until smooth. Add dill and whipping cream. Season to taste with salt and mix for 30 seconds. Cover and refrigerate until needed.

TO SERVE: Divide soup among chilled soup bowls. Garnish with salmon roe, dill and breadsticks.

1½ large long English cucumbers

1 clove garlic

2 cups/500 mL milk

2 Tbsp/30 mL chopped fresh dill

¼ cup/60 mL whipping cream

2 oz/60 g preserved salmon roe, sockeye or spring, for garnish

4 sprigs dill for garnish

8 breadsticks for garnish

Celeriac and
Smoked Black cod Potage

. . . .

1 Tbsp/15 mL unsalted butter

1 celeriac, chopped

½ onion, chopped

½ leek, white part only, sliced

1 small carrot, chopped

1 Yukon Gold potato, peeled, in
   ½-inch/1-cm cubes

1 bay leaf

3 cups/750 mL vegetable stock
   (page 163)

6 oz/170 g smoked Alaskan
   black cod

1 Tbsp/15 mL chopped fresh
   tarragon for garnish

CELERIAC IS A ROOT VEGETABLE that is not often used in British Columbia. However, it has a good earthy flavour that complements many foods, including black cod. Although you may find smoked black cod that has been artificially coloured red, I prefer to use naturally smoked fish, which is ivory in colour.

Makes 4 servings

Melt butter in a saucepan on medium heat and sauté celeriac, onion, leek and carrot for 5 minutes, until they become translucent. Turn down the heat to low and add potato. Cook for 1 minute, then add bay leaf.

Turn up the heat to medium and add stock. Bring soup to a simmer and add fish. Cook for 5 minutes, then use a slotted spoon to remove fish from soup and place it on a plate. Use a fork to separate the cod's flesh into small flakes.

Simmer soup on low heat for 40 minutes, until vegetables are cooked. Remove and discard bay leaf. Transfer soup to a blender and purée. Season to taste with salt and pepper.

TO SERVE: Pour soup into a tureen. Garnish with fish flakes and tarragon.

Manila CLAM Soup with
Madras Curry and Sea Asparagus

. . . .

MANILA CLAMS are one of the most popular varieties of clams on the West Coast. They are full of meat and are best during cold winter months.

Sea asparagus is a kind of seaweed. It is harvested all over the coast of British Columbia between the end of May and the middle of June. After this, the inside of the asparagus turns woody. Try to find fresh sea asparagus, as frozen sea asparagus is not as juicy. If fresh sea asparagus is not available, substitute dried seaweed or fresh green asparagus.

Makes 4 servings

Wash clams well.

Melt 1 Tbsp/15 mL of the butter in a saucepan on medium heat. Stir in curry paste. Add shallots, leek, tomato and celery, then cook for 5 minutes, until the vegetables become soft and translucent. Add clams and sauté for 1 minute. Stir in wine, thyme and bay leaf. Cover the pot with a lid and cook for 5 minutes, until the shells open. Use a slotted spoon to remove clams. Remove meat from the clams and save meat and juices. Discard shells and bay leaf. Reserve curried vegetables.

Melt the rest of the butter in another saucepan on medium heat and stir in flour. Stir, turn down the heat and cook for 1 minute, making sure flour does not colour. Add the curried vegetables and the reserved clam juice. Mix well, then add stock and cook for 10 minutes. Stir in whipping cream and cook for 2 minutes. Allow to cool for 10 minutes, then pour into a blender and mix for 1 minute.

Strain soup through a sieve into a clean saucepan on medium heat and bring to a boil. Cook for 1 minute. Remove and discard the foam from the top. Add sea asparagus and cook for 1 minute. Add clam meat. Cook for 1 minute more.

TO SERVE: Pour soup into a tureen and sprinkle with cilantro and parsley.

1½ lbs/680 g Manila clams
¼ cup/60 mL butter
1 Tbsp/15 mL Madras curry paste
3 shallots, thinly sliced
1 leek, white part only, thinly sliced
1 tomato, thinly sliced
1 stalk celery, thinly sliced
1 cup/250 mL Chardonnay
1 sprig fresh thyme, chopped
1 bay leaf
3 Tbsp/45 mL all-purpose flour
2 cups/500 mL fish stock (page 162)
1 cup/250 mL whipping cream
½ cup/125 mL fresh sea asparagus
1 Tbsp/15 mL sliced fresh cilantro
    for garnish
1 sprig fresh parsley, chopped,
    for garnish

Chilled AVOCADO Soup with
Dungeness Crabmeat and Jalapeño Sorbet

. . . .

*T*HE TARTNESS of the sorbet and the richness of the avocado give this chilled soup an interesting complexity of flavour and texture. You can make the sorbet a day ahead and keep it in the freezer, but you should make the soup only an hour before, or the avocado will turn black. If you don't have a deep-fryer, use crumbled blue corn chips as a garnish instead of the tortillas. If you don't have an ice cream maker, you can use store-bought lemon sorbet. Make sure the sorbet is not too sweet.

Makes 4 servings

SORBET: Cut jalapeño pepper in half. Remove and discard the seeds from one half; leave the seeds in the other half.

Combine the jalapeño pepper half that has the seeds with sugar, water and lemon juice in a saucepan on medium heat, then bring to a boil for 1 minute. Remove from heat and allow to cool. Remove and discard jalapeño pepper and seeds. Stir in tequila and a pinch of salt.

Transfer to a blender, add the remaining jalapeño pepper half without the seeds, and purée.

Pour the mixture into an ice cream maker. Process according to the manufacturer's directions until set, then place sorbet in the freezer for 1 hour. Make 4 scoops and keep on a tray in the freezer until needed.

GARNISH: Preheat oil in a deep fryer to 300°F/150°C. Deep-fry the tortillas one at a time, for 5 seconds, until soft. Place each deep-fried tortilla between two small ladles for 2 minutes to shape it into a cup. Fry the formed tortillas for 2 minutes more, then drain on paper towels.

SOUP: Peel avocados, then remove and discard pits. Cut into quarters and place them in a blender. Add stock and lime juice. Purée until the mixture has a smooth consistency. Add half of the whipping cream and mix briefly. Season to taste with salt and pepper.

TO SERVE: Divide soup among chilled soup bowls. Garnish with crabmeat and cilantro. Put a scoop of jalapeño sorbet into each tortilla cup and place one in the centre of each bowl. Drizzle 1 Tbsp/15 mL of the remaining whipping cream on each serving.

SORBET

1 jalapeño pepper

2 Tbsp/30 mL sugar

1 cup/250 mL water

3 lemons, juice of

1 oz/30 mL tequila

GARNISH

8 cups/2 L canola, peanut or
    sunflower oil for deep-frying

4 blue corn tortillas, each
    4 inches/10 cm in diameter

SOUP

3 avocados

½ cup/125 mL vegetable stock
    (page 163)

1 lime, juice of

½ cup/125 mL whipping cream

2 oz/60 g Dungeness crabmeat
    for garnish

1 Tbsp/15 mL chopped fresh
    cilantro for garnish

Corn and Elephant GARLIC Soup
with Chipotle Pepper

. . . .

1 ear corn

3 cloves elephant garlic, peeled

1 Tbsp/15 mL olive oil

1 shallot, thinly sliced

½ leek, julienned

½ canned chipotle pepper
   (about 1 tsp/5 mL)

1 Yukon Gold potato, peeled, in
   1½-inch/3.5-cm cubes

4 cups/1 L vegetable stock (page 163)

2 cups/500 mL soy milk

Pinch of ground cumin for garnish

1 Tbsp/15 mL fresh cilantro leaves
   for garnish

*T*HIS IS A SIMPLE SOUP with a bit of a kick. I make it in the fall because I love the smoky taste of the chipotle pepper. If fresh corn is not available, you can substitute frozen. You can also use regular garlic in place of the elephant garlic.

If you like, you can make a double batch. Any leftover soup will keep in the refrigerator for 4 days or frozen in an airtight container for up to 2 weeks.

Makes 4 servings

Shuck the corn and use a knife to cut off corn kernels; save kernels and discard cob. Cut each garlic clove in two, then remove and discard the centre germs.

Heat olive oil in a saucepan on medium-low heat. Sauté corn, garlic, shallot, leek and chipotle pepper without colouring for 7 minutes, until translucent. Add potato, stock and soy milk, then cook for 20 minutes, until fork-tender.

Transfer to a blender and mix until smooth. Place in a clean saucepan on medium heat and bring to a boil.

TO SERVE: Pour soup into heated serving bowls and garnish with ground cumin and cilantro.

*J*HIS SOUP IS a Cannery classic. Be careful not to over-roast the lobster shells, or the soup will be bitter-tasting. Just before serving the bisque, bring it to boil on medium heat and mix with a hand-held blender for 20 seconds. This will emulsify the liquid and give the bisque a velvety texture.

Makes 4 servings

Preheat the oven to 375°F/190°C. Heat a roasting pan in the oven for 5 minutes. Add olive oil and lobster shells. Roast in the oven for 30 minutes.

Add carrot, onion, shallots, celery, tomato and garlic to the roasting pan. Add tomato paste and toss gently. Return the roasting pan to the oven for 15 minutes.

Remove the pan from the oven and place on the stove on medium heat. Add cognac and deglaze the pan, then step back from the stove and carefully light the cognac. Let the flame die down, then transfer contents to a saucepan on medium heat. Sprinkle flour over lobster shells, stir well and cook for 2 minutes. Add wine and cook for 2 minutes. Add stock and bouquet garni, then cook for 30 minutes. Remove and discard bouquet garni.

Use a slotted spoon to transfer lobster shells and vegetables to a food processor, leaving the stock in the saucepan. Mix shells and vegetables for 30 seconds, until they form a smooth paste. Return this mixture to stock, stir in whipping cream and cayenne, then cook for 5 minutes.

Strain stock through a sieve into a clean blender. Discard solids. Allow stock to cool for 30 minutes to avoid burning yourself when mixing. Remove and discard stems from tarragon. Chop tarragon leaves, then stir into strained stock and season to taste with salt and pepper. For a stronger flavour, add a drop of cognac. Purée soup, transfer to a saucepan on medium heat and bring to a boil.

TO SERVE: Divide among warmed soup bowls.

1 Tbsp/15 mL olive oil

2 lbs/900 g lobster (or crab or prawn) shells

½ carrot, in ¼-inch/5-mm cubes

½ onion, in ¼-inch/5-mm cubes

2 shallots, in ¼-inch/5-mm cubes

1 stalk celery, in ¼-inch/5-mm cubes

1 tomato, in ¼-inch/5-mm cubes

3 cloves garlic, in ¼-inch/ 5-mm cubes

1 Tbsp/15 mL tomato paste

2 Tbsp/30 mL cognac

1½ Tbsp/25 mL all-purpose flour

1 cup/250 mL Sauvignon Blanc

3 cups/750 mL fish stock (page 162)

1 bouquet garni (page 15)

½ cup/125 mL whipping cream

Pinch of cayenne pepper

2 sprigs fresh tarragon

FISH & SHELLFISH

ENTRÉES

. . . .

*A*T THE CANNERY,

we are proud to offer a large selection of

fish and shellfish and to be one of the

leading seafood restaurants in Vancouver.

We serve fish caught on the West Coast, across Canada

and around the world. Some are popular varieties,

and others are less-known species such as skate,

idiot fish or walleye. When it is available,

you will also find freshwater fish on the menu.

Grilled Albacore TUNA
with Anchovies, Capers and
Black Olive Butter

. . . .

BLACK OLIVE BUTTER

8 oz/225 g unsalted butter, room
temperature

Pinch of freshly ground black pepper

2 Tbsp/30 mL 10-year-old balsamic
vinegar or reduce ¼ cup/60 mL
regular balsamic vinegar to half

5 fillets anchovy

2 Tbsp/30 mL black olives, pitted

2 Tbsp/30 mL capers

1 Tbsp/15 mL chopped fresh basil

TUNA

¼ cup/60 mL olive oil

2 cloves garlic

1 Tbsp/15 mL chopped fresh parsley

4 pieces albacore tuna, each
7 oz/200 g

4 slices old-fashioned country bread

WE DON'T USE albacore tuna as often as Ahi tuna because it is too soft for many dishes and because most of it is frozen at sea, but it is still a great fish to grill. Albacore is available between August and November. Serve this tuna dish with a trio of grilled bell peppers (green, red and yellow) or a mixed green salad, and save some of the black olive butter to use with other grilled dishes. It will keep in the refrigerator, covered with plastic wrap, for 4 days.

Makes 4 servings

BLACK OLIVE BUTTER: Place butter, a pinch of freshly ground black pepper and balsamic vinegar in a blender or food processor. Mix for 2 minutes. Add anchovies and mix for 10 seconds. Add olives, capers and basil, then mix for 15 seconds.

TUNA: Preheat the grill or barbecue to medium.

Make a coulis by mixing olive oil, garlic and parsley in a blender for 1 minute. Transfer to a shallow bowl.

Season tuna with salt and pepper and place in the coulis, turning fish to make sure it is evenly coated. Allow to marinate for 5 minutes. Grill fish for 2 minutes, then turn over and cook for 2 minutes (for rare). (Personally I like my tuna rare. You may have to adjust the cooking time depending on the thickness of the fish and how well cooked you like it.)

TO SERVE: Grill bread slices on both sides. Spread black olive butter on one side of the bread. Place a piece of tuna and a slice of grilled buttered bread on each warmed serving plate.

Crispy-skinned Spring SALMON
with Snap Peas and
Summer Truffle Vinaigrette

. . . .

*T*HIS IS ONE of my favourite salmon dishes. The idea is to cook the salmon very slowly, skin side down, so the heat penetrates the fish slowly, leaving more moisture and flavour. The crispy skin gives this dish great contrast. Any salmon would work, but I prefer spring salmon for its taste, moisture and oil content.

If you can't find truffles, use 2 Tbsp/30 mL truffle oil or basil–olive oil vinaigrette and reduce the quantity of vegetable oil to ⅓ cup/75 mL.

Makes 4 servings

VINAIGRETTE: Wash truffle under running water and brush it gently to remove any dirt. Pat truffle dry with a paper towel and cut into quarters.

Place shallot, Dijon mustard, port, sherry vinegar and salt in a blender. Mix well. With the motor running, slowly add oil. Add truffle and mix for 5 seconds.

SALMON AND SNAP PEAS: Fill a saucepan three quarters full of water and stir in salt. Bring to a boil on high heat, add snap peas and cook for 2 minutes. Transfer to a colander and run cold water over peas in order to stop the cooking. Drain and set aside.

Season salmon with salt and pepper. Heat olive oil in a non-stick frying pan on medium heat. Sear salmon, skin side down, for 1 minute. Turn down the heat to low and cook for 18 minutes. White creamy pearls will appear on the fish when it is done.

While the fish is cooking, melt half of the butter in another frying pan on medium heat. Sauté snap peas for 2 minutes until warm. Add the remaining butter, parsley and water (to create steam). Cover the pan with a lid to keep peas warm.

TO SERVE: Divide snap peas among 4 warmed plates and place a salmon fillet, skin side up, on top of each. Drizzle vinaigrette over salmon and garnish with a sprinkle of fleur de sel.

VINAIGRETTE
⅓ oz/10 g small fresh
   summer truffle
½ small shallot
1 Tbsp/15 mL Dijon mustard
½ cup/125 mL ruby port, reduced
   to ¼ cup/60 mL
2 Tbsp/30 mL sherry vinegar
½ tsp/2.5 mL salt
½ cup/125 mL vegetable oil

SALMON AND SNAP PEAS
2 tsp/10 mL salt
1 lb/450 g snap peas
4 fillets spring salmon, each
   7 oz/200 g
1 Tbsp/15 mL olive oil
2 Tbsp/30 mL butter
1 Tbsp/15 mL chopped fresh parsley
1 Tbsp/15 mL water
Fleur de sel for garnish

Cedar-planked ARCTIC CHAR with Summer Berry Relish

. . . .

2 Tbsp/30 mL hazelnut oil

1 onion, chopped

1 green onion, sliced

½ cup/125 mL brown sugar

½ cup/125 mL balsamic vinegar

1 tomato, in ¼-inch/5-mm dice

1 bay leaf

Pinch of freshly ground nutmeg

½ cup/125 mL raspberries

½ cup/125 mL blueberries

½ cup/125 mL blackberries

½ cup/125 mL blackcurrants

1 Tbsp/15 mL chopped fresh cilantro

4 Arctic char fillets, each 7 oz/200 g

I PREFER TO USE FRESH FISH in season and cook it medium-rare to retain both the moisture and the flavour. This is a great summer dish, especially when served with young tender greens drizzled with hazelnut oil. In the winter, use fresh fish from the Great Lakes or the Yukon or Northwest Territories and berries that have been frozen IQF (individual quick frozen). Salmon or trout would be good alternatives to Arctic char.

Be sure to use an untreated 8- to 10-inch/20- to 25-cm cedar plank free of chemicals—you can find one at a specialty cookware store.

Makes 4 servings

Soak the cedar plank overnight in a bucket of water.

Heat 1 tsp/5 mL of the hazelnut oil in a saucepan on medium heat. Sauté onion and green onion for 2 minutes, or until translucent. Stir in brown sugar and cook for 1 minute. Stir in balsamic vinegar, tomato, bay leaf and nutmeg, then cook for 5 minutes. Turn down the heat to low and stir well. Add raspberries, blueberries, blackberries and blackcurrants, then cook for 5 minutes. Add cilantro. Season to taste with salt and pepper. Remove from the heat and allow to cool.

Transfer to a covered container and refrigerate until needed. (This berry relish can be made a day ahead and will keep for up to 3 days in the refrigerator.)

Preheat the oven to 375°F/190°C. Remove the cedar plank from the water and pat it dry with a dish towel. Use a pastry brush to apply a thin coat of the remaining hazelnut oil to the plank. Place fish, skin side down, on the plank. Season fish with salt and pepper. Roast in the oven for about 10 minutes, until creamy "pearls" appear on the flesh.

TO SERVE: Present fish on the plank with berry relish on the side.

Roasted Sockeye SALMON with
Pinot Noir Demi-glace and
Sautéed Spinach with Garlic Chips

. . . .

DEMI-GLACE

4 tsp/20 mL butter

1 cup/250 mL thinly sliced shallots

2 cups/500 mL Pinot Noir

1 cup/250 mL fish stock (page 162)

3 cups/750 mL brown chicken stock
   (page 164)

1 sprig fresh thyme, chopped

½ tsp/2.5 mL crushed black pepper

SALMON

6 cloves garlic

1 cup/250 mL milk

3 Tbsp/45 mL olive oil

4 fillets sockeye salmon,
   each 7 oz/200 g

4 slices bacon

2 lbs/900 g young spinach leaves

Pinch of sugar

2 Tbsp/30 mL butter

SOCKEYE SALMON is leaner than spring salmon, so I like to add flavour and moisture by wrapping it in bacon. The bacon will also protect the flesh during cooking. I use chicken stock to add a nice consistency to my sauce, as using only wine and fish stock would make the sauce gritty and too light. You can use veal stock instead of the chicken stock.

Makes 4 servings

DEMI-GLACE: Melt 1 tsp/5 mL of the butter in a saucepan on medium heat and sauté shallots for 5 minutes, until golden. Add wine and cook until reduced to one quarter, about 5 minutes. Stir in fish stock and cook until reduced to one quarter, about 15 minutes. Turn up the heat to high, stir in chicken stock and thyme, then cook until reduced to half, about 20 minutes.

Strain sauce through a sieve into a clean saucepan, discarding solids. Place the saucepan on low heat. Stir in black pepper, the remaining butter and salt to taste.

SALMON: Preheat the oven to 375°F/190°C. Line a cookie sheet with parchment paper.

Use a Japanese mandoline to cut garlic into very thin slices. Place garlic and milk in a bowl and let soak for 1 hour. Use a slotted spoon to remove garlic and drain on paper towels. Discard milk. Toss garlic with 1 Tbsp/15 mL of the olive oil in a bowl. Arrange garlic on the cookie sheet and bake for 30 minutes. (Do not overcook garlic, or it will taste bitter.) Remove garlic from the oven and season to taste with salt and pepper. Leave the oven on.

Cut each salmon fillet in half but do not cut through the skin. Fold each fillet in half, skin sides facing in. Wrap bacon around salmon and secure it with a wooden toothpick or butcher's string. Season with salt and pepper on both sides.

Heat 1 Tbsp/15 mL of the olive oil in an ovenproof frying pan on medium heat. Sauté salmon for 20 seconds on each side. Roast in the oven for 10 minutes.

While salmon is cooking, heat the remaining olive oil in another frying pan on high heat. Sauté spinach for 1 minute (a lot of water will come out). Sprinkle with sugar and cook for 1 minute. Drain spinach in a colander. Set the frying pan aside.

TO SERVE: In the frying pan in which you cooked spinach, melt butter on medium heat. Turn up the heat to high, return spinach to the pan and cook for 1 minute, until warm.

Reheat the sauce. Arrange salmon and spinach on a warmed serving platter. Sprinkle with garlic chips and spoon warm sauce onto the platter beside the salmon and spinach.

Fricassée of CRAYFISH with Sautéed Fiddleheads

. . . .

CRAYFISH

4 lbs/1.8 kg live crayfish

1 Tbsp/15 mL vegetable oil

6 Tbsp/90 mL butter

2 shallots, chopped

⅓ cup/75 mL cognac

1 Tbsp/15 mL tomato paste

½ cup/125 mL all-purpose flour

1 cup/250 mL Chardonnay

1 tsp/5 mL crushed black pepper

2 bay leaves

¼ tsp/1 mL cayenne pepper,
   or to taste

5 cups/1.25 L fish stock (page 162)

FIDDLEHEADS

4 cups/1 L fresh or frozen
   fiddleheads

½ tsp/2.5 mL salt

2 Tbsp/30 mL butter

1 shallot, chopped

1 Tbsp/15 mL chopped fresh chives

1 tsp/5 mL chopped garlic

I CONSIDER CRAYFISH to be the lobster of lakes and rivers because, though it is much less expensive than lobster, it is still a delicacy. If you have lots of time and patience, try catching them yourself. If you buy them at the market, look for live, brightly coloured crayfish with hard shells.

Fiddleheads are available early in the spring; they are also sold frozen. You can use yellow wax beans or chard instead.

Makes 4 servings

CRAYFISH: Place crayfish in a colander and rinse under cold running water.

Heat vegetable oil and butter in a large saucepan on medium heat. Sauté shallots for 2 minutes, until translucent. Add crayfish, cover with a lid and cook for 2 minutes, until shells begin to turn red. Add cognac, stand back from the stove and carefully light cognac with a match. Let flame die down, then stir in tomato paste and cook for 1 minute. Slowly stir in flour and cook for 1 minute. Add wine, black pepper, bay leaves and cayenne pepper; bring to a boil. Add stock, cover with a lid and cook for 5 minutes.

Use a slotted spoon to transfer crayfish to a warmed plate. Cook and reduce stock on low heat for 15 minutes.

FIDDLEHEADS: Wash fiddleheads well in cold water, then trim off and discard any blackened stems.

Fill a saucepan with hot water and salt. Place on high heat and bring to a boil. Add fiddleheads and cook for 2 minutes, until al dente. Drain in a colander.

Melt butter in a frying pan on medium heat. Sauté shallot for 1 minute. Add fiddleheads, chives and garlic; reheat for 1 minute until hot.

TO SERVE: Spoon reduced stock onto a warmed serving platter. Place crayfish in the stock. Arrange fiddleheads beside them.

Pan-fried SKATE with Bacon and
Celery Mashed Potatoes

. . . .

PAN-FRYING is a good way to prepare skate. We serve it with especially flavourful potatoes from the Pemberton Valley north of Whistler. The celery and bacon go very well with these potatoes.
Makes 4 servings

POTATOES: Fill a saucepan with water, stir in a pinch of salt and add potatoes. Bring to a boil on medium heat and cook for 20 minutes, until fork-tender. Drain in a colander and transfer to a kitchen mixer with a paddle attachment.

Melt 1 Tbsp/15 mL of the butter in a nonstick frying pan on medium heat and sauté bacon for 2 minutes, until translucent. Add shallots and cook for 2 minutes, until translucent.

In another saucepan on medium heat, combine milk, whipping cream, garlic and the rest of the butter, then bring to a boil. Add bacon-shallot mixture and celery leaves. Pour into the potatoes in the kitchen mixer and process for 1 minute.

SKATE: Preheat the oven to 375°F/190°C. Season fish with salt and pepper.

Add a drop of olive oil to an ovenproof frying pan on medium heat and cook fish for 1 minute. Add 1 Tbsp/15 mL of the unsalted butter and cook for 1 minute. Turn fish over and cook in the oven for 2 minutes (depending on the thickness of the fish), until clear juice appears on the flesh. Transfer fish to a warmed platter.

To the pan in which you cooked the fish, add shallots and sauté on medium heat for 3 minutes, until light golden. Add port and cook until reduced to half, about 5 minutes. Add stock and cook until reduced to half, about 5 minutes. Stir in salted butter, then season to taste with salt and pepper. Strain sauce through a sieve into a clean saucepan on low heat to warm it up.

TO SERVE: Place a piece of fish and a dollop of mashed potatoes on each of 4 warmed serving plates. Stir sage and the remaining unsalted butter into the sauce and serve it in a bowl on the side.

POTATOES

1½ lbs/680 g Pemberton or
   Yukon Gold potatoes, in 2-inch/
   5-cm cubes
2 Tbsp/30 mL butter
4 oz/115 g bacon, in ¼-inch/
   5-mm dice
3 shallots, sliced
½ cup/125 mL milk
½ cup/125 mL whipping cream
2 cloves garlic, chopped
1 Tbsp/15 mL celery leaves, chopped

SKATE

1 skate wing with bone or ling cod,
   in 4 pieces, each 200 g/7 oz
Drop of olive oil
2 Tbsp/30 mL unsalted butter
1 Tbsp/15 mL chopped shallot
½ cup/125 mL ruby port
1 cup/250 mL brown chicken stock
   (page 164)
2 Tbsp/30 mL salted butter
1 tsp/5 mL chopped fresh sage

Poached SKATE with
Caper and Lemon Black Butter

. . . .

SKATE IS BECOMING more and more popular. Cook the fish the same day you buy it, or it will develop a lemony flavour. The wings of the skate are the only part of the fish that has meat, and I prefer to use small skate wings and cook them with the bone in because the meat is more delicate.

This is a straightforward recipe that you can make with any white fish. Dress it up with fresh herbs or substitute balsamic vinegar for the raspberry vinegar.

Makes 4 servings

SKATE: Place court bouillon in a large saucepan on medium heat and bring to a boil. Cook for 10 minutes. Add fish, cover with a lid and cook for 4 minutes. Drain fish and place a piece on each warmed serving plate.

GARNISH: Fill a large saucepan with hot water. Add olive oil and salt, then bring to a boil on high heat. Add pasta and cook for 2 minutes. Drain in a colander and rinse with cold running water, then return to the same saucepan over high heat. Add butter, tomatoes and basil, then toss gently. Set aside.

BLACK BUTTER: Melt butter in a frying pan on high heat until foamy. Stir in capers, lemon and balsamic vinegar, then add tarragon and anchovies.

TO SERVE: Pour black butter mixture over skate and place some fettuccine on the side of each serving.

SKATE

8 cups/2 L court bouillon (page 163)

1 skate wing with bone or ling cod,
    4 pieces, each 200 g/7 oz

GARNISH

1 Tbsp/15 mL olive oil

½ tsp/2.5 mL salt

9 oz/250 g fresh fettuccine

1½ tsp/7.5 mL butter

2 tomatoes, peeled, deseeded, in
    ¼-inch/5-mm dice

1 Tbsp/15 mL chopped fresh basil

BLACK BUTTER

3 Tbsp/45 mL butter

2 Tbsp/30 mL small capers

1 lemon, peeled and cut into
    ½-inch/1-cm dice

⅓ cup/75 mL balsamic vinegar

1 Tbsp/15 mL chopped fresh tarragon

2 fillets anchovy, diced

Fresh WALLEYE with Sun-dried Tomato and Olive Mashed Potatoes and Watercress Coulis

. . . .

POTATOES

½ cup/125 mL sun-dried tomatoes

1½ lbs/680 g Yukon Gold potatoes

1 tsp/5 mL salt

⅔ cup/150 mL whipping cream

1 Tbsp/15 mL butter

½ cup/125 mL olive oil

1 tsp/5 mL chopped garlic

⅓ cup/75 mL pitted black olives

COULIS

1 bunch fresh watercress

Drop of white wine vinegar

1 Tbsp/15 mL butter

2 shallots, chopped

1 cup/250 mL fish stock (page 162)

1 cup/250 mL whipping cream

¼ cup/60 mL Noilly Prat or other
   white vermouth

½ tsp/2.5 mL sugar

½ lemon, juice of

2 Tbsp/30 mL chopped fresh basil

FISH

4 fillets walleye or lake trout,
   each 7 oz/200 g

Drop of olive oil

WALLEYE IS ONE of the tastiest fish from the lakes of eastern Canada. If walleye is not available, you can substitute any white fish or salmon. The mashed potatoes complement this dish very well. I like to use olive, hazelnut, lobster, walnut or truffle oil to give the mashed potatoes a special flavour. When making the coulis, be careful not to overcook the green vegetables or herbs, otherwise they will become an unappetizing dark colour.

Makes 4 servings

POTATOES: Place sun-dried tomatoes in a bowl of warm water, cover and let soak for 2 hours. Drain and coarsely chop the tomatoes.

Peel potatoes and cut into quarters. Fill a saucepan with cold water, stir in salt and add potatoes. Cook on medium heat for 20 minutes, until fork-tender.

COULIS: Cut off and discard large stems from watercress. Place the leaves in a bowl of cold water with a drop of vinegar for 2 minutes. Drain on paper towels.

Melt half of the butter in a saucepan on medium heat. Sauté shallots for 2 minutes, until translucent. Add stock and cook until reduced to half, about 5 minutes. Stir in whipping cream and Noilly Prat, then cook for 2 minutes. Stir in the remaining butter and set aside.

FINISH POTATOES: When potatoes are cooked, drain and place in a kitchen mixer with a paddle attachment. Heat whipping cream and butter in a saucepan on high heat until hot. Add hot cream mixture to potatoes, then mix slowly. Add sun-dried tomatoes, olive oil, garlic and olives. Season to taste with salt and pepper. Mix for 1 minute. Set aside and keep warm.

FINISH COULIS: Place sauce back on medium heat and bring to a boil. Add watercress, sugar and lemon juice. Allow to cool for 10 minutes, then transfer to a blender or food processor; mix well for 10 seconds. Add basil. Season to taste with salt and pepper. Mix for 5 seconds, then pour back into the saucepan. Reheat gently.

FISH: Preheat the oven to 375°F/190°C. Season fish with salt and pepper.

Heat a drop of olive oil in an ovenproof frying pan on medium heat, then sauté fish fillets for 2 minutes. Turn fish over and bake in the oven for about 2 minutes (depending on the thickness of the fillets), until creamy "pearls" appear on the flesh. Drain fish on paper towels.

TO SERVE: Divide mashed potatoes among 4 warmed plates. Place a piece of fish beside each serving of potatoes. Serve warmed sauce in a separate bowl on the side.

DOGFISH Tandoori with Cardamom Basmati Rice and Tomato Chutney

. . . .

CHUTNEY

1 Tbsp/15 mL olive oil

½ red bell pepper, in ¼-inch/
5-mm cubes

½ green bell pepper, in ¼-inch/
5-mm cubes

½ red onion, in ¼-inch/5-mm cubes

1 stalk celery, in ¼-inch/5-mm cubes

½ cup/125 mL brown sugar

½ cup/125 mL balsamic vinegar

1 tsp/5 mL mustard seeds

2 tomatoes, in ¼-inch/5 mm-cubes

½ jalapeño pepper, deseeded

1 bay leaf

1 green onion, sliced

1 Tbsp/15 mL chopped fresh cilantro

1 Tbsp/15 mL chopped fresh parsley

TANDOORI

4 shallots, sliced

2 Tbsp/30 mL tandoori paste

1 tsp/5 mL toasted ground cumin
(page 91)

2 lbs/900 g dogfish or shark or
marlin, in 1-inch/2.5-cm cubes

1 tsp/5 mL olive oil

2 limes, juice of

1 cup/250 mL fresh cilantro,
leaves only

RICE

1 tsp/5 mL olive oil

½ cup/125 mL onion, chopped

3 green cardamom pods, crushed

2 cups/500 mL basmati rice

3 cups/750 mL water

1 tsp/5 mL butter

*T*HIS IS A SPECIALTY of our morning chef, Eddy Geekiyanage, who is from Sri Lanka. If dogfish is unavailable, you can make this recipe with any other firm fish, including shark, marlin, tuna or king mackerel. Make the chutney ahead of time, transfer it to an airtight container and reserve for up to 10 days, until needed. This chutney goes well with any curry dish.

Makes 4 servings

CHUTNEY: Heat olive oil in a saucepan on medium heat. Sauté red and green bell peppers, red onion and celery for 4 minutes, until light golden. Stir in brown sugar and cook for 4 minutes, until completely dissolved. Add balsamic vinegar and cook until reduced to half, about 5 minutes. Add mustard seeds, tomatoes, jalapeño pepper and bay leaf, then cook for 15 minutes, until vegetables are soft. Add green onion, cilantro and parsley, then cook for 1 minute. Season to taste with salt and pepper. Remove from heat and allow to cool.

TANDOORI: Combine shallots, tandoori paste and ground cumin in a bowl. Add fish and toss gently to coat evenly. Cover and marinate in the refrigerator for 2 hours.

RICE: Heat olive oil in a saucepan on medium heat. Sauté onion and cardamom for 2 minutes, until translucent. Add rice and stir well. Add water, cover with a lid and cook for 15 minutes, until water has completely evaporated. Stir in the butter.

FINISH TANDOORI: Remove fish and shallots from marinade and pat dry. Discard marinade. Heat olive oil in a frying pan on high heat. Sauté fish and shallots for 2 minutes, until shallots become translucent. Turn down the heat to medium. Season to taste with salt and pepper, then stir in lime juice and half of the cilantro.

TO SERVE: Arrange fish on a warm serving platter. Sprinkle with the remaining cilantro, and serve with some tomato chutney on the side. Place the rice in a separate serving bowl.

HALIBUT Steamed with Lapsang Souchong Tea, Sweet and Sour Sauce

· · · · · · · · · · ·

*L*APSANG TEA FROM CHINA has a unique smoky flavour that's a good complement to halibut. Tea is being used more and more in cooking, as Asian influences fuse with West Coast cooking. You can use this same method with chicken or pork.

Makes 4 servings

SAUCE: Peel and julienne ginger; save the trimmings. Cut off and save big stems of cilantro. Roughly chop leaves.

Heat sesame oil in a saucepan on medium heat, then sauté ginger and shallots, stirring well, for 1 minute. Add brown sugar and cook for 1 minute. Add pineapple juice, cook for 1 minute, then add rice vinegar. Bring to a boil and turn down the heat to low.

Mix water and cornstarch together in a small bowl, then pour slowly into the sauce, stirring all the while. Cook for 1 minute. Season to taste with salt and pepper. Add chili pepper. Turn off the heat. Stir in green onion and cilantro leaves.

HALIBUT: Grind tea leaves to a powder in a coffee grinder or spice mill. Season halibut with salt, pepper and powdered tea.

Place a medium saucepan with 1 inch/2.5 cm water on medium heat. Add cilantro stems and ginger trimmings. Bring to a boil.

Place halibut in a 9-inch/22.5-cm bamboo steamer, covered with a lid, on top of the pot of boiling water. Steam fish for about 6 minutes (depending on the thickness), until creamy "pearls" appear on the flesh.

While fish is cooking, heat sesame oil in a frying pan on high heat. Add bok choy and oyster sauce, cover with a lid and cook for 2 minutes, until soft but still green. Add sesame seeds, chopped garlic and soy sauce. Season to taste with salt and pepper.

TO SERVE: Divide bok choy among 4 warmed plates and place a piece of halibut on the side of each. Serve with warm sauce in a sauceboat on the side.

SAUCE

1 oz/30 g fresh ginger, a 2-inch/ 5-cm piece

1 cup/250 mL chopped fresh cilantro

1 Tbsp/15 mL sesame oil

2 shallots, thinly sliced

2 Tbsp/30 mL brown sugar

¾ cup/175 mL pineapple juice

⅓ cup/75 mL rice vinegar

¼ cup/60 mL water

1 Tbsp/15 mL cornstarch

1 red chili pepper, deseeded and chopped

1 green onion, thinly sliced

HALIBUT

1 Tbsp/15 mL Lapsang Souchong tea leaves

4 fillets halibut, each 7 oz/200 g

1 tsp/5 mL sesame oil

1 lb/450 g bok choy

1 Tbsp/15 mL oyster sauce

1 tsp/5 mL toasted sesame seeds

¼ tsp/1 mL chopped garlic

1 Tbsp/15 mL soy sauce

Lavender-crusted HALIBUT with
Raspberry Sauce and Pea Shoot Salad

. . . .

CRUST

1 Tbsp/15 mL lavender

1½ tsp/7.5 mL fresh parsley

½ cup/125 mL dried bread crumbs

1 Tbsp/15 mL olive oil

SAUCE

½ cup/125 mL butter, melted

1 shallot, chopped

¼ cup/60 mL ruby port

1 cup/250 mL raspberries

Pinch of crushed black pepper

1 cup/250 mL whipping cream

2 egg yolks

HALIBUT

4 fillets halibut, each 7 oz/200 g

1 Tbsp/15 mL olive oil

SALAD

3 cups/750 mL pea shoots or
   mesclun

1 tsp/5 mL blackberry vinegar or
   raspberry vinegar

1 Tbsp/15 mL walnut oil or
   olive oil

*W*E MAKE THIS RECIPE from March through November, when halibut is in season. The lavender enhances the flavour of the halibut, but you can vary the fish or the herb used in the crust. Try sole, snapper or cod with the lavender, or tarragon, anise seed or dried powdered mushrooms with the halibut.

Makes 4 servings

CRUST: Combine lavender, parsley and bread crumbs in a food processor. Mix for 1 minute, then add olive oil. Mix briefly. Season with salt and pepper, then set crust aside to dry for 1 day.

SAUCE: Heat 1 tsp/5 mL of the butter in a saucepan on medium heat and sauté shallot for 2 minutes, until translucent. Deglaze the pan with port and cook until reduced to half, about 1 minute. Turn down the heat to low. Add raspberries and pepper, then cook for 5 minutes. Add two thirds of the whipping cream and cook for 2 minutes.

Transfer sauce to a blender or food processor and mix well. Strain through a sieve to remove berry seeds. Clean the blender or food processor and put the sauce back in it. Process on medium speed for 10 seconds. Mix in egg yolks one by one, then slowly add the rest of the melted butter. Season to taste with salt.

HALIBUT: Preheat the oven to 375°F/190°C. Season halibut with salt and pepper.

Heat olive oil in an ovenproof frying pan on medium heat, then sear halibut for 1 minute. Turn fish over and place lavender crust mixture on top. Bake in the oven for about 3 minutes, until golden (depending on the thickness of halibut).

SALAD: While halibut is cooking, toss pea shoots, blackberry vinegar and walnut oil in a bowl. Season to taste with salt and pepper.

TO SERVE: Finish the sauce by bringing the remaining whipping cream to a boil in a saucepan on medium heat, whisking constantly. Reduce the heat to low and slowly stir in the sauce. Mix well.

Divide salad among 4 plates. Remove halibut from the oven, drain on paper towels and place one fillet on each plate. Pour a pool of warm sauce on the side of each plate.

RED SNAPPER "en Papillote" with Thai Basil

. . . .

4 lbs/1.8 kg whole red snapper,
   cleaned and scaled

1 lb/450 g mussels

2 Tbsp/30 mL olive oil

1 onion, julienned

1 carrot, julienned

1 leek, white part only, julienned

1 stalk celery, julienned

2 Tbsp/30 mL butter

1 cup/250 mL Sauvignon Blanc

1 cup/250 mL fresh Thai basil

"*E*N PAPILLOTE" is a quick and easy way to cook a whole fish over the barbecue or in the oven. Traditionally, the papillote is made with waxed paper, but it is better to use aluminum foil at home. Wrap the fish in foil, cook it, and when you open the foil bag, the aromas will surround you. You can also cook this dish on a barbecue on medium heat, with the cover down. If you do, reinforce the bottom of the pouch by adding extra foil.

You can make this recipe with any fish, and rather than cooking the fish whole, you can use fillets, which take less time to cook. I use Thai basil because it imparts a stronger flavour than regular basil, but let taste be your guide.

Makes 4 servings

Preheat the oven to 375°F/190°C.

Rinse fish under running water and drain on paper towels. Wash mussels, making sure to remove and discard their beards.

Cut 3 sheets of aluminum foil, each 12 × 24 inches/30 × 60 cm. Join 2 sheets, shiny side in, along the 24-inch/60-cm side by folding the edges together to make a long rectangular sheet 22 × 24 inches/ 55 × 60 cm. Turn the third sheet so that the 24-inch/60-cm side is parallel to the 22-inch/55-cm side of the large sheet. Place the third sheet on top of the other two, making sure that it covers and reinforces the seam of the big sheet. Fold the edges up slightly, then drizzle the foil with olive oil.

Place fish on the foil and season with salt and pepper. Place mussels, onion, carrot, leek, celery, butter, wine and Thai basil on fish. Fold the four corners of the foil to the centre and twist closed so that you have an airtight pouch. Place the foil pouch on a cookie sheet and bake in the oven for 30 minutes. Remove from the oven and place on a serving platter.

TO SERVE: Carefully open the pouch (the steam is very hot).

Roasted KOKANEE TROUT with Cèpes Mushrooms and Hazelnut Butter Cream Sauce

. . . .

KOKANEE TROUT is similar to salmon. It is a wild fish with a very delicate flesh. Since you can't find it at the market, buy a fly-fishing rod with a "Carey special" fly and catch it yourself.

Using a ceramic dish for this recipe will yield better-tasting fish, because it spreads heat evenly across its entire surface.

Makes 4 servings

Preheat the oven to 375°F/190°C.

Heat vegetable oil in a frying pan on high heat. Sauté mushrooms and thyme for 2 minutes, until soft. Drain in a colander.

Heat an ovenproof ceramic plate in the oven for 5 minutes. Season trout with salt and pepper. Remove the heated plate from the oven and place 4 Tbsp/60 mL of the butter on it. Place fish on the plate and roast in the oven for about 10 minutes (for whole medium fish), until golden. Baste fish a few times during cooking. Halfway through the cooking time, add half of the shallots to the butter in the dish.

When fish is almost done, sprinkle with lemon juice. Remove from the oven, transfer fish to a platter and keep warm. Save the plate and turn down the oven temperature to 225°F/110°C.

To make the sauce, pour wine into the ceramic plate and return to the oven for 2 minutes. Transfer the liquid from the plate to a saucepan on medium heat. Stir in whipping cream and bring to a boil. Transfer to a blender and mix for 1 minute while slowly adding hazelnut oil. Continue to mix for 30 seconds, until sauce becomes smooth. Season with salt and pepper.

To finish the mushrooms, melt the remaining butter in a clean frying on medium heat until it turns golden brown. Cook the mushrooms for 4 minutes, until soft. Add the remaining shallots, parsley, garlic and 1 Tbsp/15 mL of the chives. Season to taste with salt and pepper.

TO SERVE: Gently reheat sauce and transfer to a sauceboat. Arrange fish and the mushroom mixture on 4 warmed serving plates. Garnish with hazelnuts and the remaining chives.

1 tsp/5 mL vegetable oil

2 lbs/900 g cèpes (porcini), cut in wedges

1 sprig fresh thyme, chopped

4 whole (or fillets) Kokanee trout, each 7 oz/200 g

⅓ cup/75 mL butter

4 shallots, chopped

1 lemon, juice of

½ cup/125 mL Chardonnay

1½ cups/375 mL whipping cream

⅓ cup/75 mL hazelnut oil

1 tsp/5 mL chopped fresh parsley

1 tsp/5 mL chopped garlic

3 Tbsp/45 mL chopped fresh chives

3 Tbsp/45 mL toasted and crushed hazelnuts for garnish

Grey cod Fish
and Chips with Salad

. . . .

*T*HIS IS AN ELEGANT WAY to serve fish and chips. To get a nicely textured batter, use cold eggs directly from the refrigerator and add a drop of vinegar when all the other ingredients have been mixed. It is important to refrigerate the batter for at least one hour before you use it, so the yeast can set. If cod is not available, you can also make this dish with halibut, snapper or mackerel. Serve the fish and chips with a nice cold Okanagan pale ale.

Makes 4 servings

BEER BATTER: Combine flour and chives with a pinch of salt in a large bowl. Make a hole in the middle. Put egg yolks in the hole and beat into the flour with a whisk. Add milk and mix. Slowly pour in the beer, mixing constantly. Cover and refrigerate for 2 hours.

FISH AND CHIPS: Heat oil in a deep fryer to 300°F/150°C. Cut cod into strips 5 inches/12.5 cm long and 1½ inches/3.5 cm wide.

Peel potato, taro and lotus root, then slice thinly, using a mandoline, to make chips. Rinse slices in a colander under running water to remove the starch. Drain on paper towels.

Place one handful of slices at a time in the deep fryer, stirring well with the skimmer, and cook for about 2 minutes until soft. Drain on paper towels and season with salt. When all the slices are cooked, turn up the heat of the deep fryer to 350°F/180°C.

In a bowl, whip egg whites until firm. Add vinegar, then whip a few minutes more. Fold into the batter and mix well.

Dip fish strips into the batter one at a time. Deep-fry for 4 to 6 minutes, until the batter turns golden. When all the fish strips are cooked, turn up the heat of the deep fryer to 375°F/190°C. Add chips and deep-fry a second time for about 3 minutes, until golden and crispy. Drain on paper towels.

SALAD: Place mesclun in a salad bowl with walnut oil and malt vinegar. Toss gently and season to taste with salt and pepper.

TO SERVE: Add chips to salad and toss gently to avoid breaking the chips. Place the cooked fish in a basket or individual martini glasses lined with parchment paper. Serve with lemon wedges in a bowl on the side.

BEER BATTER

1 cup/250 mL all-purpose flour

1 Tbsp/15 mL chopped chives

2 egg yolks

½ cup/125 mL milk

½ cup/125 mL pale ale

FISH AND CHIPS

8 cups/2 L vegetable oil for
 deep-frying

4 grey cod fillets, each 8 oz/
 225 g, deboned

1 large Yukon Gold potato

1 small taro root (page 96)

1 lotus root

2 egg whites

Drop of white vinegar or lemon juice

SALAD

6 oz/170 g mesclun or micro greens

¼ cup/60 mL walnut oil

2 Tbsp/30 mL malt vinegar

1 lemon, cut in wedges, for garnish

Smoked SABLEFISH and Savoy Cabbage
with Chive Crème Fraîche

. . . .

CHIVE CRÈME FRAÎCHE
⅔ cup/150 mL whipping cream

2 tsp/10 mL buttermilk

1 lemon, juice of

⅓ cup/75 mL sour cream

2 Tbsp/30 mL chopped fresh chives

FISH AND CABBAGE
2 Tbsp/30 mL salt

1 Savoy cabbage

2 Tbsp/30 mL butter

2 shallots, chopped

7 oz/200 g diced bacon, in
 ½-inch/1-cm cubes

1 sprig fresh thyme, chopped

1 bay leaf

½ cup/125 mL fish stock (page 162)

1 cup/250 mL whipping cream

4 pieces smoked sablefish, each
 7 oz/200 g

2 Tbsp/30 mL chopped
 fresh parsley

*S*AVOY CABBAGE, also known as *chou frisé,* has a nice mild flavour that goes very well with smoked sablefish. I like the idea of mixing hot and cold food, and here the hot smoked sablefish and the cool fresh crème fraîche go well together. Make this dish to celebrate a special occasion.

Makes 4 servings

CHIVE CRÈME FRAÎCHE: Combine whipping cream and buttermilk in a bowl. Cover and leave at room temperature for 30 hours. The cream will thicken.

Gently whisk in lemon juice, sour cream and chives. Season with freshly ground black pepper to taste. Cover and refrigerate until needed.

FISH AND CABBAGE: Preheat the oven to 350°F/180°C. Fill a saucepan with water and add salt. Place on high heat and bring to a boil.

While water is heating, cut cabbage into quarters. Remove and discard the hard core in the middle. Cut cabbage into very thin slices and rinse in cold water. When the water is boiling, add cabbage and cook for 1 minute. Drain in a colander and cool down with cold running water to stop the cooking.

Melt butter in an ovenproof saucepan on medium heat. Sauté shallots, bacon, thyme and bay leaf for 2 minutes, until shallots are translucent. Add precooked cabbage, stock and whipping cream. Cook for 1 minute. Add smoked sablefish and cover the pot with a lid. Bake in the oven for 15 to 20 minutes, until creamy "pearls" appear on the flesh.

Remove from the oven and transfer fish to a warmed plate. Pick out and discard bay leaf. Add parsley to the cabbage mixture and mix well.

TO SERVE: Place cabbage mixture in the middle of 4 warmed serving plates and top each with a piece of fish. Serve crème fraîche in a small bowl on the side.

Cornmeal-crusted BRILL Fillets with Avocado-Tomato Salsa

. . . .

*T*HIS DISH is a nice light, easy summer recipe. For variety, replace the brill with sole or snapper and substitute passion fruit, pineapple or mango for the avocado in the salsa.

To toast cumin, place cumin seeds in a frying pan on medium heat and sauté, stirring constantly, for 5 minutes. The seeds should be lightly toasted. Once the seeds have cooled, grind them in a coffee grinder for about 30 seconds. Will keep for up to 7 days in an airtight container.

Makes 4 servings

SALSA: Combine cucumber, red and green bell peppers, tomatoes, avocado and red onion in a bowl. Add lime juice, garlic, ground cumin, olive oil, sambal oelek and half of the cilantro. Season to taste with salt and pepper. Mix well, cover and refrigerate until needed.

FISH: Season sole with salt and pepper, then coat with cornmeal. Heat butter and olive oil in a nonstick pan on medium heat. When butter is foamy, cook fish for 2½ minutes. Turn over, and cook for 2½ minutes (depending on the thickness of the fillets), until golden brown. Drain on paper towels.

TO SERVE: Place a piece of fish on each of 4 plates. Spoon some salsa on the side. Sprinkle with the remaining cilantro.

SALSA

½ long English cucumber, deseeded, in ¼-inch/5-mm cubes

½ red bell pepper, deseeded, in ¼-inch/5-mm cubes

½ green bell pepper, deseeded, in ¼-inch/5-mm cubes

2 tomatoes, in ¼-inch/5-mm cubes

1 avocado, peeled and pitted, in ¼-inch/5-mm cubes

¼ red onion, in ¼-inch/5-mm cubes

1 lime, juice of

2 cloves garlic, chopped

½ tsp/2.5 mL toasted ground cumin

¼ cup/60 mL olive oil

¼ tsp/1 mL sambal oelek, or to taste

2 Tbsp/30 mL chopped fresh cilantro

FISH

4 fillets brill, each 7 oz/200 g

½ cup/125 mL cornmeal

4 Tbsp/60 mL butter

2 Tbsp/30 mL olive oil

Chilled Nova Scotia LOBSTER and Crispy Pickled Cucumbers with Dill and Lemon Balm Cream Sauce

. . . .

LOBSTER

24 cups/6 L court bouillon (page 163)

4 whole live lobsters, each
1¼ lbs/570 g

SALAD

3 long English cucumbers

½ cup/125 mL rice vinegar

1 Tbsp/15 mL coarse sea salt

½ cup/125 mL sour cream

⅔ cup/150 mL whipping cream

1 Tbsp/15 mL chopped pickled ginger

1½ tsp/7.5 mL chopped fresh dill

1½ tsp/7.5 mL chopped fresh
lemon balm

*T*HIS IS A VERY NICE, refreshing way to serve Nova Scotia lobster. You can also serve prawns, crab or Caribbean lobster this way. Do not use frozen lobster; though live ones are more expensive, the quality is far superior. Do not precook or overcook lobster, or it will become chewy.

Makes 4 servings

LOBSTER: Place court bouillon in a stockpot on high heat and bring to a simmer for 5 minutes. Add lobsters, cover with a lid and cook for about 12 minutes.

Remove lobsters from the pot and let them cool down. Discard court bouillon.

Cut cooked lobsters in half lengthwise and crack open the claws using the back of a heavy knife. Place in a container and refrigerate for up to 4 hours until needed.

SALAD: Cut cucumbers in half lengthwise. Remove and discard seeds, then cut into ¼-inch/5-mm cubes. Combine rice vinegar and sea salt in a bowl and add cucumber. Cover and marinate in the refrigerator for 40 minutes.

Drain cucumber in a colander and discard the marinade. Place cucumbers on paper towels to dry.

Combine cucumber, sour cream, whipping cream, pickled ginger, dill and lemon balm in a bowl. Season to taste with salt and pepper.

TO SERVE: Place each lobster, meat side up, on a serving plate. Serve the salad in bowls on the side.

Blackened SWORDFISH with
Mild Creole Sauce and
Rosemary-roasted Sweet Potatoes

. . . .

*S*WORDFISH CAN BE FOUND in many areas of the Pacific Ocean. It has a meaty texture, and I like to spice it up. You can buy a premixed Cajun spice in specialty stores, but I prefer to make my own mix of 3 Tbsp/45 mL paprika, 1 Tbsp/15 mL onion powder, 1 Tbsp/15 mL dried marjoram, 1 tsp/5 mL black pepper, 1 tsp/5 mL garlic powder, 1 tsp/5 mL dried sage and ½ tsp/2.5 mL cayenne, all mixed together in a coffee grinder. This mix will keep in an airtight container for up to 3 weeks.

You can also serve the creole sauce with pork, roast chicken or, if you are brave, alligator. Substitute white chicken stock for the fish stock, if you use meat or chicken.

Makes 4 servings

FISH: Rub swordfish with Cajun spice. Place in a bowl, cover and refrigerate until needed.

SAUCE: Heat olive oil in a saucepan on medium heat. Sauté bell pepper, celery, onion, carrot, chili pepper, okra, bacon, garlic and bay leaf for 4 minutes, until vegetables are soft. Stir in tomato paste and cook for 1 minute. Add wine and cook, stirring, for 1 minute. Add stock and tomatoes. Turn down the heat to low and cook for 20 minutes, until sauce begins to thicken. Season to taste with salt and pepper.

SWEET POTATOES: Preheat the oven to 375°F/190°C. Heat olive oil in an ovenproof frying pan on medium heat and sauté sweet potatoes for 2 minutes. Place in the oven and roast for 20 minutes, mixing every 5 minutes, until sweet potatoes are cooked. Take the pan out of the oven, leaving the oven on to finish the fish, and place on the stove on low heat. Add rosemary, butter and honey, toss together, and cook for 2 minutes. Place on a warmed serving platter.

FINISH FISH: Heat olive oil in an ovenproof pan on medium-high heat. Sear swordfish for 1½ minutes. Turn fish over and place the pan in the oven for 3 minutes, until golden brown. Drain on paper towels.

TO SERVE: Arrange fish on the same serving platter as sweet potatoes. Gently heat the sauce and serve in a sauceboat on the side.

FISH

4 pieces swordfish, each 7 oz/200 g
1 Tbsp/15 mL Cajun spice mix
1 tsp/5 mL olive oil

SAUCE

1 tsp/5 mL olive oil
½ red bell pepper, in ⅛-inch/ 2-mm cubes
1 stalk celery, in ⅛-inch/2-mm cubes
½ onion, in ⅛-inch/2-mm cubes
½ carrot, in ⅛-inch/2-mm cubes
1 small red chili pepper, in ⅛-inch/ 2-mm cubes
4 ⅛-inch/2-mm slices okra
½ cup/125 mL sliced bacon
2 cloves garlic, chopped
1 bay leaf
1 Tbsp/15 mL tomato paste
¼ cup/60 mL Chardonnay
2 cups/500 mL fish stock (page 162)
3 tomatoes, in ⅛-inch/2-mm cubes

SWEET POTATOES

1 tsp/5 mL olive oil
1½ lbs/680 g sweet potatoes, in 1-inch/2.5-cm cubes
1 tsp/5 mL chopped fresh rosemary leaves
1 Tbsp/15 mL butter
1 tsp/5 mL liquid honey

Oven-baked ROCKFISH and
Sautéed Provençale Vegetables
with Harissa Sauce

. . . .

SAUCE

½ cup/125 mL olive oil

½ cup/125 mL canola oil

3 egg yolks

1 Tbsp/15 mL Dijon mustard

½ lemon, juice of

¼ tsp/1 mL pesto

1 tsp/5 mL harissa paste

VEGETABLES

2 tsp/10 mL olive oil

1 bulb fennel, in ¼-inch/5-mm cubes

2 tomatoes, in ¼-inch/5-mm cubes

1 small red onion, in ¼-inch/
   5-mm cubes

1 zucchini, in ¼-inch/5-mm cubes

1 red bell pepper, in ¼-inch/
   5-mm cubes

1 green bell pepper, in ¼-inch/
   5-mm cubes

½ eggplant, in ¼-inch/5-mm cubes

¼ cup/60 mL capers

8 cherry tomatoes

8 baby yellow squash

½ cup/125 mL pitted niçoise olives

2 cloves garlic, chopped

Pinch of saffron

FISH

6 Tbsp/90 mL olive oil

1 whole rockfish, 4 lbs/1.8 kg

2 sprigs fresh thyme, chopped

2 sprigs fresh basil, chopped

COOKING THE FISH WHOLE is very simple; however, you must remove the scales before cooking it. Use a scallop shell or the back of a knife to scrape the scales off the fish and remember that it is a sign of freshness if the scales are difficult to remove. Or, ask your fish shop to clean and descale the fish. Also ask the fish seller to butterfly the fish, leaving the head and tail attached. Cut out any remaining large bones and remove pin bones with tweezers. Try this recipe with perch, grouper, snapper or idiot fish.

Makes 4 servings

SAUCE: Combine olive oil and canola oil in a bowl. Place egg yolks and Dijon mustard in a food processor, then mix for 30 seconds. With the motor running, slowly add combined oils until the consistency becomes nice and thick. Add lemon juice and mix for 10 seconds. Add pesto and harissa paste, then mix for 10 seconds. Season to taste with salt and pepper.

VEGETABLES: Heat olive oil in a frying pan on high heat and sauté each vegetable individually, as some cook more quickly than others. As each vegetable is done, transfer it to the same saucepan. Add capers, olives, garlic and saffron, then cook on high heat for 2 minutes, until soft. Keep warm.

FISH: Preheat the oven to 375°F/190°C. Pour 2 Tbsp/30 mL of the olive oil onto a large ovenproof ceramic plate and place fish on it, skin side down. Season to taste with salt and pepper. Sprinkle with thyme and basil. Drizzle the remaining olive oil over fish and bake in the oven for 15 minutes, until the flesh flakes from the bone and the juice runs clear.

TO SERVE: Carefully transfer the whole fish to a warmed serving platter and arrange the warm vegetables beside the fish. Serve the cold harissa sauce in a bowl on the side.

Giant SCALLOPS and Seared
Quebec Foie Gras with Fig Molasses

. . . .

SAUCE

1 tsp/5 mL butter

2 shallots, chopped

⅓ cup/75 mL ruby port

½ cup/125 mL fish stock (page 162)

1 cup/250 mL brown chicken
　　stock (page 164)

VEGETABLES

8 cups/2 L vegetable oil for
　　deep-frying

1 large manioc or taro root

1 tsp/5 mL salt

10 oz/285 g green beans
　　(about 2 cups/500 mL)

1 tsp/5 mL butter

1 Tbsp/15 mL chopped fresh parsley

SCALLOPS AND FOIE GRAS

16 giant scallops, U-10, each 2 oz/
　　60 g (page 3)

4 pieces fresh duck foie gras,
　　each 2 oz/60 g

⅓ cup/75 mL all-purpose flour

1 tsp/5 mL salted butter

Drop of vegetable oil

⅓ cup/75 mL fig molasses or honey

1 tsp/5 mL unsalted butter

*T*HE DIFFERENT FLAVOURS and textures of this dish—the sweetness of the scallops, the richness of the foie gras and the crispiness of the manioc (or taro)—are a great combination.

Manioc, also known as cassava or yucca, is a root vegetable native to South America. Taro root is a potato-like vegetable that is native to India and parts of southeastern Asia. Some varieties of both manioc and taro are toxic when raw, so be sure to cook them thoroughly.

Makes 4 servings

SAUCE: Melt butter in a saucepan on medium heat and sauté shallots for 3 minutes, until golden. Add port and cook until reduced to half, about 3 minutes. Add fish stock and cook for another 3½ minutes, until reduced to one third. Add chicken stock and cook a further 5 minutes, or until reduced to half.

VEGETABLES: Preheat oil in a deep fryer to 350°F/180°C.

Peel and cut manioc into strips 2 inches/5 cm × ½ inch/1 cm × ½ inch/1 cm (just like thick french fries). Precook in the deep fryer for 4 minutes, until soft. Use a slotted spoon to transfer manioc to a plate. Leave deep fryer on.

Fill a large saucepan two thirds full of hot water and add salt. Place on high heat and bring to a boil. Add green beans and cook for 5 minutes, until al dente. Drain in a colander and cool down with cold running water to stop the cooking.

SCALLOPS AND FOIE GRAS: Remove tendons from scallops (the firm white part attached to the flesh). Pat scallops dry with paper towels, then season with salt and pepper.

Season foie gras with salt and pepper on both sides and coat evenly with flour (this will protect foie gras during cooking). Shake gently to get rid of excess flour.

Heat salted butter and a drop of vegetable oil in a nonstick frying pan on medium heat. Sauté scallops for 2 minutes on each side, until golden. Transfer scallops to a warmed plate. Turn up the heat to high and sauté foie gras for 1 minute on each side, until golden. Place foie gras beside the scallops on the warmed plate.

Discard half of the butter from the frying pan. Stir in fig molasses and the reserved sauce. Bring to a boil on medium heat and add the unsalted butter. Strain sauce through a sieve into a clean saucepan and discard solids.

FINISH VEGETABLES: Place green beans and butter in a saucepan on medium heat and heat for 2 minutes, until hot. Add the parsley.

Cook manioc in the deep fryer for 1 minute, until light golden. Drain on paper towels and season with salt.

TO SERVE: Arrange scallops, foie gras, green beans and manioc on 4 warmed serving plates, with warm sauce in a bowl on the side.

Dungeness CRAB with
Fermented Chinese Black Beans

. . . .

4 live Dungeness crabs, each
   1¾ lbs/800 g
2 Tbsp/30 mL sesame oil
2 green onions, thinly sliced
½ cup/125 mL fermented Chinese
   black beans, rinsed
½ cup/125 mL julienned ginger
1 Tbsp/15 mL sugar
1 tsp/5 mL toasted sesame seeds
¼ cup/60 mL soy sauce
1¼ cups/300 mL fish stock
   (page 162)
1 Tbsp/15 mL cornstarch
3 Tbsp/45 mL water
½ bunch fresh cilantro, chopped

WE MAKE OUR OWN fermented black beans by marinating fresh black beans in salt and water with a little ground ginger and then letting them dry in the sun for a few days. Once bottled, they will keep for up to a year. Or, you can buy fermented black beans and fermented black bean paste at Asian food stores. I prefer the whole beans to the paste because they have a fuller flavour and firmer texture. Steamed jasmine rice and some sautéed Chinese long beans (page 102) complement this dish nicely.

Makes 4 servings

Cut each live crab into four quarters. Heat sesame oil in a wok or frying pan on high heat and sauté crab for 2 minutes, until the shell begins to turn red. Add green onions, fermented black beans and ginger. Cover with a lid, turn down the heat to low and cook for 2 minutes, until crab is bright red. Add sugar and sesame seeds. Stir in soy sauce and stock, then cook for 5 minutes. Season to taste with salt and pepper.

Mix cornstarch and water in a cup. While whisking constantly, slowly add cornstarch mixture to bouillon. Stir in cilantro.

TO SERVE: Place crab on a long, deep serving plate. Serve rice and vegetables in separate bowls on the side.

cod Tongue Fritters

. . . .

THIS DISH IS VERY POPULAR in eastern Canada, but on the west coast it is a real delicacy. Cod tongues have a soft texture and a delicate flavour, and I prefer them to halibut cheeks. Eat these with your fingers, accompanied by a glass of cold pale ale. Or, eat them pan-fried and finished with garlic butter and lemon juice.

Makes 4 servings

TARTAR SAUCE: Whisk together egg yolks, Dijon mustard, salt and pepper in a bowl. While whisking constantly, slowly add sunflower oil. Whisk until the consistency becomes thick, then stir in lemon juice. Mix in capers, gherkins, shallot, parsley and chives. Cover and refrigerate until needed, up to 1 or 2 days.

FRITTERS: Separate eggs, placing yolks and whites in 2 different bowls.

Place flour in a bowl and make a hole in the middle. Place egg yolks in the hole. While whisking gently, add milk slowly (to avoid lumps). Slowly pour in beer, mixing constantly. Cover and refrigerate for 2 hours.

Preheat oil in a deep fryer to 350°F/180°C.

Place egg whites in a kitchen mixer with a whisk attachment and mix for 2 minutes, until volume has tripled and egg whites are frothy. Add a pinch of salt and increase the speed for about 1 minute, until egg whites become foamy. Whisk in lemon juice to make egg whites firm. Use a spatula to very gently fold egg whites into fritter batter.

Pat cod tongues dry with paper towels, then season with salt and pepper. Dip into batter and deep-fry for 3 minutes, until golden. Drain on paper towels.

SALAD: Place mesclun, sorrel, nasturtium flowers and leaves in a bowl. Add mussel vinaigrette and toss gently.

TO SERVE: Place fritters and salad on 4 serving plates, with tartar sauce in a bowl on the side.

TARTAR SAUCE
2 egg yolks
1 Tbsp/15 mL Dijon mustard
1 cup/250 mL sunflower oil
½ lemon, juice of
1 Tbsp/15 mL capers
2 Tbsp/30 mL chopped gherkins
1 Tbsp/15 mL chopped shallot
1 Tbsp/15 mL chopped fresh parsley
1 Tbsp/15 mL chopped fresh chives

FRITTERS
2 eggs
1 cup/250 mL all-purpose flour
½ cup/125 mL milk
½ cup/125 mL pale ale
8 cups/2 L vegetable oil for
 deep-frying
½ lemon, juice of
1½ lbs/680 g cod tongues or halibut
 cheeks or small snapper fillets

SALAD
8 oz/225 g mesclun
1 cup/250 mL fresh young
 sorrel leaves
2 cups/500 mL fresh nasturtium
 flowers and leaves
½ cup/125 mL creamy mussel
 vinaigrette (page 166)

Prosciutto and Basil-wrapped
KING CRAB Tempura with Asparagus

. . . .

I RECOMMEND USING the meat from the "merus," which is the largest section of a crab leg, as it is the easiest to work with. If you buy fresh king crab from a fish market, you will have to poach it first in court bouillon; most packaged crab is precooked. You can also substitute black cod or salmon for the king crab, and beer batter (page 89) for the tempura.

Makes 4 servings

TEMPURA BATTER: Combine rice flour, cornstarch and sesame seeds in a bowl. While whisking constantly, slowly add sesame oil and ice water. Cover and refrigerate for 2 hours.

SAUCE: Whisk together egg yolks and Dijon mustard in a bowl. Season to taste with salt and pepper. While whisking constantly, slowly add vegetable oil. Whisk until sauce becomes thick. Stir in pickled ginger and soy sauce.

ASPARAGUS AND CRAB: Preheat oil in a deep fryer to 375°F/190°C.

Fill a saucepan with water, add salt and bring to a boil on high heat. Cook asparagus for about 2 minutes (depending on the thickness of the stalks), until al dente. Drain on paper towels and keep warm.

Arrange 4 prosciutto slices side by side on a cutting board. Place 2 sections of crabmeat and a few basil leaves in the middle of each slice. Add a third leg on top, followed by another slice of prosciutto. Tightly roll up prosciutto around crab legs, trimming crab if necessary to match the length of prosciutto, to make 4 rolls.

Add two ice cubes to the tempura batter. Dip the rolls in tempura batter and deep-fry for 3 minutes until crispy. Drain on paper towels.

TO SERVE: Arrange 4 pieces of asparagus on each warmed serving plate. Cut crab rolls in half, then arrange them over the asparagus. Serve sauce in a bowl on the side.

TEMPURA BATTER

1 cup/250 mL rice flour or all-
purpose flour

1 cup/250 mL cornstarch

1 Tbsp/15 mL toasted sesame seeds

1 Tbsp/15 mL sesame oil

2¾ cups/675 mL ice water

2 ice cubes

SAUCE

3 egg yolks

1 Tbsp/15 mL Dijon mustard

1 cup/250 mL vegetable oil

1 Tbsp/15 mL chopped pickled ginger

1 Tbsp/15 mL soy sauce

ASPARAGUS AND CRAB

8 cups/2 L vegetable oil or canola oil
or peanut oil for deep-frying

1 tsp/5 mL salt

10 oz/285 g asparagus, peeled
and trimmed

8 thin slices prosciutto

20 oz/570 g king crab merus
sections, without the shell, each
about 4 inches/10 cm long

½ cup/125 mL fresh basil leaves

Dungeness CRAB with Ginger–Soy Butter
and Green Papaya Salad

. . . .

CRAB

24 cups/6 L court bouillon (page 163)

4 live Dungeness crabs or live
   lobsters, each 1½ lbs/680 g

SAUCE

⅔ cup/160 mL unsalted butter,
   in 1-inch/2.5-cm cubes, room
   temperature

2 shallots, chopped

1 Tbsp/15 mL pickled ginger

⅓ cup/75 mL rice vinegar

½ tsp/2.5 mL sambal oelek

1 tsp/5 mL honey

⅓ cup/75 mL soy sauce

⅓ cup/75 mL whipping cream

SALAD

½ tsp/2.5 mL salt

1 cup/250 mL Chinese long beans,
   in 2-inch/5-cm lengths

2 lbs/900 g green papaya

2 green onions, sliced

2 shallots, sliced

2 cloves garlic, chopped

1 small hot green chili pepper,
   chopped

2 Tbsp/30 mL brown sugar

1 Tbsp/15 mL Thai fish sauce

⅓ cup/75 mL lime juice

⅓ cup/75 mL crushed roasted
   peanuts

2 Tbsp/30 mL chopped dried shrimp

½ cup/125 mL mint leaves

GREEN PAPAYA SALAD is a traditional Thai dish. You can use green mango instead, if you wish.

Chinese long beans are also called string beans, and you can find them in Asian markets all year round. You can cook them the same way as green (or French) beans, or sauté them with oil in a wok the Asian way.

Makes 4 servings

CRAB: Bring court bouillon to a boil in a stockpot on medium heat. Cook for 5 minutes. Add crabs, cover with a lid and cook for about 21 minutes, until shells turn bright red. Remove crabs from the pot and discard bouillon.

SAUCE: Melt 1 tsp/5 mL of the unsalted butter in a saucepan on medium heat. Sauté shallots and pickled ginger for 2 minutes, until translucent. Add rice vinegar, sambal oelek, honey and soy sauce. Cook for about 5 minutes, until reduced to half. Stir in whipping cream and cook until reduced to half, another 5 minutes. Turn down the heat to low and slowly whisk in the rest of the butter. Season to taste with salt and pepper. Strain sauce through a sieve into a clean saucepan.

SALAD: Fill a saucepan with water, add salt and bring to a boil on high heat. Cook long beans for 1 minute. Drain in a colander and cool under running water to stop the cooking.

Peel green papaya, then cut in half. Remove and discard seeds. Julienne using a Japanese mandoline and place in a large bowl. Add blanched long beans, green onions and shallots, then toss together.

Place garlic, chili pepper, brown sugar, fish sauce and lime juice in a mortar, and crush together. Pour over papaya salad and toss together.

TO SERVE: Place dressed salad on a serving platter and sprinkle with peanuts, shrimp and mint. Arrange the crab on the side. Reheat sauce and serve on the side in small bowls.

IDIOT FISH Roasted with Fennel
and Thyme, and Provençale Tomatoes

. . . .

IDIOT FISH is not very well known, but it has a very delicate texture and is one of my favourites. I like to serve the fish whole so that it can be shared at the table. If you prefer using fillets, be sure to precook the fennel in a frying pan before placing it in the oven with the fish.

Makes 4 servings

FISH AND VEGETABLES: Preheat the oven to 375°F/190°C.

Cut tomatoes in half, then season with salt and pepper. Combine garlic, parsley, bread crumbs and melted butter in a bowl. Place the bread mixture on top of tomato halves.

Cut fennel in half. Remove and discard the hard part in the middle. Cut into thin slices and arrange in a roasting pan or on an ovenproof ceramic plate. Sprinkle with 2 Tbsp/30 mL of the olive oil. Season with salt and pepper.

Place fish on top of fennel, add wine, then season with salt and pepper. Scatter thyme sprigs on top of fish. Bake in the oven for 15 minutes. Place tomato halves around fish and top each half with the remaining olive oil and a dab of butter. Return to the oven and bake for 15 minutes, until creamy "pearls" appear and the flesh flakes from the bone.

SAUCE: Peel and cut lemons into ¼-inch/5-mm cubes. Discard the peel. Melt 1 tsp/5 mL of the unsalted butter in a saucepan on low to medium heat. Sauté lemons, shallots and thyme for 2 minutes, until shallots are translucent. Add wine and cook until liquid is reduced to almost none.

Turn up the heat to high, stir in whipping cream and bring to a boil. Turn down the temperature to low. While whisking slowly, add butter cubes one at a time. The sauce should not exceed 120°F/50°C, otherwise it will split. (If the sauce does split, bring ¼ cup/60 mL whipping cream to a boil in a saucepan. Slowly whisk the split sauce into the boiling cream, a bit at a time, until the sauce is fully incorporated.)

TO SERVE: Place fish on a warmed serving platter, then arrange tomatoes and fennel around it. Serve the sauce in a sauceboat on the side.

FISH AND VEGETABLES

4 Roma tomatoes

3 cloves garlic, chopped

2 Tbsp/30 mL chopped fresh parsley

⅓ cup/75 mL dried bread crumbs

1 Tbsp/15 mL butter, melted

2 bulbs fennel

3 Tbsp/45 mL olive oil

1 whole idiot fish or snapper,
    4 lbs/1.8 kg, or 2 fillets,
    each 2 lbs/900 g

⅓ cup/75 mL Chardonnay

1 cup/250 mL sprigs fresh thyme

2 tsp/10 mL butter

SAUCE

2 lemons

8 oz/225 g unsalted butter,
    in 1-inch/2.5-cm cubes, room
    temperature

3 shallots, chopped

1 sprig fresh thyme

½ cup/125 mL Chardonnay

⅓ cup/75 mL whipping cream

Sautéed PRAWNS and FROG LEGS
with Parsley-Garlic Cream Sauce and
Goat Cheese Mashed Potatoes

. . . .

MASHED POTATOES

1¾ lbs/800 g Yukon Gold potatoes,
   peeled, in 1-inch/2.5-cm cubes

1 cup/250 mL whipping cream

½ cup/125 mL milk

¼ cup/60 mL chopped sun-dried
   tomatoes

1½ tsp/7.5 mL chopped garlic

2 oz/60 g soft goat cheese

2 Tbsp/30 mL extra-virgin olive oil

FROG LEGS AND PRAWNS

8 frog legs, each pair 1½ oz/45 g

16 spot prawns, heads on

1 Tbsp/15 mL all-purpose flour

1 Tbsp/15 mL olive oil

1 Tbsp/15 mL butter

1 shallot, chopped

½ cup/125 mL Chardonnay

1 cup/250 mL fish stock (page 162)

1 cup/250 mL whipping cream

½ clove garlic, chopped

3 Tbsp/45 mL fresh Italian flat-leaf
   parsley leaves

½ lemon, juice of

4 sprigs fresh parsley for garnish

*F*ROG LEGS AND PRAWNS go very well together, because the
delicate texture of the frog legs complements the sweetness
of the spot prawns. Both are enhanced by the green garlic sauce.
If you don't like frog legs, you can still make this dish with just spot
prawns or black tiger prawns.

Makes 4 servings

MASHED POTATOES: Fill a saucepan with cold water, add a pinch of
salt and potatoes. Bring to a boil on medium heat and cook for about
20 minutes, until fork-tender.

While potatoes are cooking, make the tomato-cream mixture.
Combine whipping cream, milk, sun-dried tomatoes and garlic in a
saucepan on medium heat and bring to a simmer. Cook for 3 minutes.

Drain potatoes, place in a kitchen mixer with a whisk attachment
and mix slowly for 2 minutes. Pour hot tomato-cream mixture slowly
over potatoes, mixing gently. Keep mixing while slowly adding goat
cheese and olive oil. Season to taste with salt and pepper.

FROG LEGS AND PRAWNS: Season frog legs and prawns with salt and
pepper. Coat frog legs with flour. Heat olive oil in a nonstick frying
pan on medium heat and sauté frog legs for 2 minutes, until cooked.
Add 1 tsp/5 mL of the butter and sauté prawns for 2 minutes, until
they begin to turn red. Remove frog legs and prawns from the pan.

To make the sauce, place shallot in the same pan on medium
heat and sauté for 1 minute, until translucent. Add wine and cook
until reduced to one quarter, about 3 minutes. Add stock, whipping
cream and garlic and cook until reduced to half, about 7 minutes. Stir
in the remaining butter, then allow to cool for 10 minutes. Transfer to
a blender, add parsley leaves and lemon juice, then mix for 1 minute.

TO SERVE: Transfer sauce to a saucepan on medium heat and reheat.
If it's necessary to reheat frog legs and prawns place them in the
sauce as you reheat it.

Place mashed potatoes in the middle of a warmed serving platter,
and arrange frog legs and prawns around the edge. Garnish with
parsley sprigs. Serve the sauce on the side in a sauceboat.

FISH "Pot-au-Feu"

. . . .

8 Manila clams

8 mussels

2 carrots

2 leeks, white part only

8 oz/225 g daikon

1 lb/450 g nugget potatoes

1 celery heart

2 Tbsp/30 mL olive oil

Pinch of saffron

8 cups/2 L fish stock (page 162)

1 cup/250 mL Sauvignon Blanc

1 bay leaf

4 pieces salmon, each 2 oz/60 g

4 pieces snapper, each 2 oz/60 g

4 pieces ling cod, each 2 oz/60 g

1 live Dungeness crab, 1¾ lbs/
   800 g, cut into 4 pieces

4 pink shell scallops

4 spot prawns

1 Tbsp/15 mL chopped fresh parsley

1 tsp/5 mL chopped fresh tarragon

"POT-AU-FEU," literally "pot on fire," is a traditional dish from France, usually made with beef. It is a very flavourful comfort food to chase away the chill of winter. Fish pot-au-feu can be made with any fish and shellfish that are fresh at the market. What is most important is to cook the pot-au-feu very slowly to get a nice clear broth. Add saffron to the broth if you like, then freeze any extra broth to use as fish stock or as a base for fish sauce or soups.

Makes 4 servings

Wash clams well. Wash mussels, making sure to remove and discard their beards.

Cut carrots, leeks and daikon into strips 2 inches × ¼ inch/5 cm × 5 mm. Cut potatoes into quarters. Cut celery heart into 4 pieces (use only the tender part).

Heat olive oil and saffron in a large saucepan on medium heat. Sauté carrots, leeks, daikon, potatoes and celery heart for 2 minutes, until vegetables are soft and celery heart is translucent. Add stock, wine and bay leaf and cook for 35 minutes.

Add salmon, snapper and ling cod, then cook for 10 minutes. Add crab and cook for 4 minutes. Add clams, mussels, scallops and prawns, then cover with a lid and cook for 2 minutes, until shells open. Sprinkle with parsley and tarragon.

TO SERVE: Use a slotted spoon to transfer the fish, shellfish and vegetables to a deep serving bowl. Ladle half of the cooking juices over the fish and vegetables. Pour the remaining juices into a sauceboat and serve on the side.

LING COD with Oregon Truffle Risotto

. . . .

MANY PEOPLE think of ling cod as a common fish, but it has a delicate texture and can be very impressive when cooked to perfection. Sadly, it is becoming rare as it has been overfished.

Oregon truffles are smaller than European ones, but they have a slightly garlicky taste that is excellent in risotto. Any type of risotto rice is fine, though I prefer superfine arborio, which is available in Italian food stores.

Makes 4 servings

RISOTTO: Cut truffle in half. Julienne one of the halves, and thinly slice the other.

Melt unsalted butter in a saucepan on medium heat. Stirring constantly, sauté shallots and the julienned truffle for 2 minutes, until shallots are translucent. Still stirring, add rice and wine. Cook until liquid is reduced to one third, about 5 minutes. Stir in stock. Add whipping cream, ½ cup/125 mL at a time, waiting until liquid is absorbed before adding more. Cook until rice becomes al dente, about 10 minutes. Stir in Parmesan. Keep warm.

LING COD: Preheat the oven to 375°F/190°C. Season fish on both sides with salt and pepper.

Melt unsalted butter and a drop of olive oil in an ovenproof frying pan on medium heat, until butter foams. Sauté fish for 1 minute. Place in the oven and bake for about 2 minutes. Turn fish over and cook for 5 minutes (depending on the thickness of the fish), until creamy "pearls" appear on the flesh. Transfer fish to a warm platter.

To the same frying pan, add shallot and bay leaf and sauté for 2 minutes, until shallot is translucent. Add wine and deglaze the pan. Cook until reduced to half, about 5 minutes. Add stock and cook until reduced to two thirds, about 10 minutes. Discard bay leaf. Remove from the heat and allow to cool for 10 minutes. Transfer sauce to a blender and mix well. With the motor running, slowly pour in olive oil and lemon juice.

Transfer sauce to a clean saucepan and stir in chives. Season to taste with salt and pepper.

TO SERVE: Arrange the fish on 4 warmed plates. Place a spoonful of risotto beside each piece of fish and garnish with the sliced truffle. Reheat the sauce and serve in a sauceboat on the side.

RISOTTO

1 Oregon black truffle, brushed clean

1 Tbsp/15 mL unsalted butter

2 shallots, chopped

2 cups/500 mL superfine arborio rice

¾ cup/175 mL Pinot Gris

2 cups/500 mL fish stock (page 162)

1½ cups/375 mL whipping cream

½ cup/125 mL freshly grated
   Parmesan cheese

LING COD

4 fillets ling cod, each 8 oz/225 g

1 tsp/5 mL unsalted butter

1 shallot, chopped

1 bay leaf

½ cup/125 mL Pinot Gris

1 cup/250 mL fish stock (page 162)

⅓ cup/75 mL olive oil

½ lemon, juice of

2 Tbsp/30 mL chopped chives

Korean Pepper–seared AHI TUNA and Peanut–Rice Vinegar Cream Sauce with Sautéed Bean Sprouts and Green Onions

. . . .

*A*HI TUNA has an instantly recognizable dark ruby colour. It is mainly caught around Hawaii and shipped whole to fish markets around the world. Like any tuna, be careful not to overcook it, as it will dry out. Most of our customers actually prefer it rare.

Korean pepper is dried chili pepper in the form of powder or flakes. I use the flakes because I find the powder too strong tasting for the fish. If it is not available, you can substitute Cajun spice.

Makes 4 servings

SAUCE: Heat sesame oil in a saucepan on medium heat and sauté shallots for 5 minutes, until golden. Stir in rice vinegar and cook for 3 minutes, until reduced to half. Add stock and cook for 2 minutes. Add ginger and cook for 1 minute. Stir in peanut butter and whipping cream. Bring to a boil, then stir in sambal oelek. Remove from heat and allow to cool for 10 minutes.

Transfer sauce to a blender and mix for 1 minute. Strain through a sieve into a clean saucepan.

TUNA: Place Korean pepper on a plate and roll tuna in it, pressing in to coat well. Season to taste with salt. Heat sesame oil in a frying pan on high heat and sear tuna for 2 minutes on each side, until golden brown.

VEGETABLES: Heat sesame oil in a nonstick frying pan on high heat. Sauté bean sprouts and green onions for 1 minute, until sprouts are translucent and greens onions are soft. Season to taste with salt and pepper.

TO SERVE: Cut each piece of fish into 3 slices. Arrange tuna and vegetables on 4 warmed serving plates. Reheat the sauce and spoon some on the side of each plate.

SAUCE

1 tsp/5 mL sesame oil

2 shallots, sliced

⅓ cup/75 mL rice vinegar

1 cup/250 mL fish stock (page 162)

½ tsp/2.5 mL grated fresh ginger

⅓ cup/75 mL unsweetened smooth
    peanut butter

½ cup/125 mL whipping cream

1 tsp/5 mL sambal oelek

TUNA

1 Tbsp/15 mL Korean pepper

4 pieces Ahi tuna, each 7 oz/200 g

1 Tbsp/15 mL sesame oil

VEGETABLES

1 tsp/5 mL sesame oil

1½ lbs/680 g bean sprouts

4 green onions

MEAT, POULTRY &

VEGETARIAN ENTRÉES

. . . .

*A*T THE CANNERY,

we use the top-quality meats in our dishes.

We cook with Canadian beef that has been aged

and air-dried for at least twenty-one days.

We also use lamb, duck, quail and rabbit

in our meat dishes, depending on the season.

Although we are a seafood restaurant, we do offer

a few vegetarian options, all of them

made from flavourful organic vegetables.

Smoked Rack of LAMB with Confit Vegetables
and Whipped Chickpeas

. . . .

CHICKPEAS

2 cups/500 mL chickpeas

1 tsp/5 mL salt

1 cup/250 mL whipping cream

½ cup/125 mL milk

2 cloves garlic, chopped

6 Tbsp/90 mL butter

LAMB

4 cloves garlic, crushed

1 sprig fresh rosemary, chopped

1 sprig fresh thyme, chopped

½ tsp/2.5 mL rock salt

1 tsp/5 mL olive oil

2 racks of lamb, each 2½ lbs/1.2 kg

VEGETABLES

2 cloves garlic

1 sprig fresh rosemary, chopped

1 sprig fresh thyme, chopped

1 Tbsp/15 mL rock salt

1 zucchini, in ¼-inch/5-mm slices

1 small eggplant, in ¼-inch/
   5-mm slices

1 red bell pepper, quartered
   and deseeded

1 green bell pepper, quartered
   and deseeded

4 Roma tomatoes, peeled

4 cups/1 L olive oil to cook the
   vegetables

*T*O SMOKE THE LAMB in this recipe, a portable smoker, which is available at outdoor stores, would work well. We start cooking the smoked rack of lamb in a 350°F/180°C oven. The meat cooks gently, leaving it moist and tender with a nice smoky taste.

Makes 4 servings

CHICKPEAS: Place chickpeas in a bowl, cover with cold water and soak for 24 hours.

LAMB: Combine garlic, rosemary, thyme, rock salt and olive oil in a bowl. Spread mixture over lamb. Place in a covered pan and refrigerate for 2 hours.

Place lamb on a tray in a cold smoker and smoke for 90 minutes. Transfer to a roasting pan and refrigerate for up to 1 day. (If you reserve the lamb overnight, brush it lightly with oil, then cover meat with plastic wrap to prevent it from drying out.)

VEGETABLES: Combine garlic, rosemary, thyme and rock salt in a bowl. Add zucchini, eggplant, red and green bell peppers and tomatoes, toss gently and marinate for 1 hour. Rinse vegetables in a colander under running cold water and dry on paper towels.

Place olive oil in a saucepan on low heat. Add vegetables and simmer for 10 minutes, until soft. Use a slotted spoon to transfer vegetables to a colander. Reserve oil for pan-frying or cooking.

FINISH CHICKPEAS: Rinse soaked chickpeas in a colander under cold running water. Place them in a saucepan and cover with fresh water. Add salt and cook chickpeas on medium heat for 45 minutes, until soft (adding more water if necessary). Drain in a colander and discard cooking liquid. Transfer chickpeas to an electric mixer with a paddle attachement or a food processor and purée.

Combine whipping cream, milk and garlic in a saucepan on medium heat; bring to a boil, then cook for 2 minutes. With the motor running, slowly pour the cream mixture into the chickpeas and mix for 2 minutes. Season to taste with salt and pepper. Add the butter.

FINISH LAMB: Preheat the oven to 350°F/180°C. Season lamb with freshly ground black pepper. Return lamb to the roasting pan and roast in the oven for 15 minutes (for medium rare).

TO SERVE: Place the chickpea purée on a warmed serving platter. Delicately place the confit vegetables on the side. Carve the lamb into 16 chops and serve 4 chops per person.

Tandoori-marinated Saddle
of LAMB and Spinach
with Cilantro, Mint and Ginger Coulis

. . . .

LAMB

¼ cup/60 mL Worcestershire sauce

½ cup/125 mL tandoori paste

¼ cup/60 mL liquid honey

1 boneless saddle of lamb,
   about 2 lbs/900 g, tied with
   butcher's string

COULIS

⅓ cup/75 mL lime juice

1 cup/250 mL fresh mint, leaves only

1 Tbsp/15 mL chopped fresh ginger

1 cup/250 mL fresh cilantro,
   leaves only

½ jalapeño pepper, deseeded

¼ cup/60 mL olive oil

1 tsp/5 mL liquid honey

SPINACH

2 Tbsp/30 mL butter

Pinch of granulated sugar

2¼ lbs/1 kg spinach, destemmed

1 tsp/5 mL chopped garlic

2 Tbsp/30 mL crumbled feta cheese

WE HAVE EXCELLENT LAMB around Vancouver, especially on Saltspring Island and in the Fraser Valley. Washington produces good lamb too, but the most affordable and most available is fresh Australian lamb. Lamb from New Zealand is usually frozen and smaller.

Makes 4 servings

LAMB: Whisk together Worcestershire sauce, tandoori paste and honey in a bowl. Rub mixture into lamb. Place in a covered pan and marinate for 2 hours in the refrigerator.

COULIS: Place lime juice, mint and ginger in a blender and mix for 20 seconds. Add cilantro and mix for 1 minute. Add jalapeño pepper, olive oil and honey, then mix until smooth. Season to taste with salt and pepper.

FINISH LAMB: Preheat the oven to 350°F/180°C or preheat a barbecue grill on low. Place lamb in a roasting pan and roast in the oven (or place on the grill) for 15 minutes, until golden (for rare, longer if you like your meat well done).

SPINACH: Melt 1 tsp/5 mL of the butter and sugar in a large frying pan on high heat. Sauté spinach for 1 minute, until soft. Drain in a colander. In the same frying pan, melt the remaining butter. Add spinach, garlic and feta cheese and cook for 1 minute, until well mixed.

TO SERVE: Remove the butcher's string from the lamb. Carve lamb into 1-inch/2.5-cm slices and place on a warmed serving platter. Arrange spinach beside the lamb, and serve coulis in a sauceboat on the side.

Roasted Okanagan QUAIL
with Lentil Compote

. . . .

J LIKE TO MAKE THIS DISH on cold winter days because it is rich, simple and flavourful comfort food. To complement the wild British Columbia quail, I use small French (Puy) lentils, which are deep green in colour, retain their shape when cooked and taste great. You can also use brown lentils, but watch them closely because they cook faster and easily become mushy.

Makes 4 servings

LENTILS: Place lentils in a bowl, add cold water to cover and soak for 24 hours at room temperature.

Rinse lentils in a colander under running water. Combine lentils, onion, bay leaves, thyme and a pinch of salt in a saucepan on medium heat. Add enough cold water to cover the lentils, then cook for 15 minutes, until lentils are soft. Drain in a colander and discard cooking water, onion, bay leaves and thyme.

QUAIL: Heat butter and a drop of vegetable oil in a saucepan on medium heat. Place quail in the pan, breast side down, and cook for 1 minute, until golden. Add shallots, lardons, thyme and bay leaf, and cook for 1 minute, until golden. Turn quail over on their backs. Season to taste with salt and pepper. Add wine, deglaze and cook until reduced to half, about 1½ minutes. Add stock and bring to a boil. Turn down the heat to low, cover with a lid and cook quail for 5 minutes, until the juice runs clear when cut with a knife. Transfer quail to a plate and save the cooking juices.

FINISH LENTILS: Melt butter in a saucepan on medium heat and sauté shallots for 2 minutes, until translucent. Stir in drained lentils, whipping cream and the reserved juices from cooking quail. Cook for 2 minutes, until boiling. Season to taste with salt and pepper.

TO SERVE: Place lentils on a warmed serving platter. Arrange the quail on top.

LENTILS

1½ cups/375 mL Puy lentils

1 small onion, studded with 3 cloves

2 bay leaves

1 sprig fresh thyme, chopped

1 tsp/5 mL butter

3 shallots, chopped

1 cup/250 mL whipping cream

QUAIL

1 tsp/5 mL butter

Drop of vegetable oil

4 quail, bone in, each 5 oz/140 g

1 Tbsp/15 mL chopped shallots

2 oz/60 g lardons

1 sprig fresh thyme, chopped

1 bay leaf

½ cup/125 mL Pinot Gris

2 cups/500 mL brown chicken stock (page 164)

Roasted CAPON with
Caramelized Root Vegetables

. . . .

A CAPON IS A ROOSTER that has been castrated so that it will naturally increase in size and have meat with a juicier and more delicate texture. Capons are not easy to find in North America, so you may have to make a special request to your butcher. Capon is an excellent substitute for turkey and could be served at Christmas or Thanksgiving. You can also use a regular chicken in this recipe, but cook it for 40 minutes less than the capon.

Makes 6 servings

Preheat the oven to 375°F/190°C. Season capon inside and out with salt and pepper. Place 1 Tbsp/15 mL of the butter inside capon. Add a drop of vegetable oil to a large roasting pan and place chicken on its back in the pan. Roast in the oven for 15 minutes.

Add garlic, parsnips, beets, celeriac, pearl onions, carrots and potatoes around the capon. Roast for 25 minutes, until vegetables are well caramelized.

Add wine and deglaze the pan. Add thyme and rosemary and roast for 15 minutes, until capon is done. To check for doneness, use the tip of a knife to prick a leg. The juice that comes out should be completely clear.

To make the sauce, remove capon from the roasting pan, place on a warmed serving platter and set aside. Use a slotted spoon to transfer the caramelized vegetables to a warmed serving bowl. Place the roasting pan on the stove on medium heat and stir in stock to deglaze. Bring to a boil and simmer for 2 minutes. Strain into a clean saucepan, discarding solids. Stir in the remaining butter and season to taste with salt and pepper.

TO SERVE: Carve the capon at the table. Serve sauce in a warmed sauceboat and vegetables on the side.

5½ lbs/2.5 kg capon

4 Tbsp/60 mL butter

Drop of vegetable oil

2 cloves elephant garlic, split and germ discarded

1 lb/450 g baby parsnips, halved

1 lb/450 g golden baby beets

1 small celeriac, in 1-inch/2.5-cm cubes

4 oz/115 g pearl onions

1 lb/450 g baby carrots

1 lb/450 g baby yellow-fleshed potatoes, unpeeled

1 cup/250 mL Pinot Gris

2 sprigs fresh thyme, chopped

1 small sprig fresh rosemary

1½ cups/375 mL brown chicken stock (page 164)

Mushroom-crusted BEEF TENDERLOIN
with Gorgonzola Mashed Potatoes
and Red Wine Sauce

. . . .

MASHED POTATOES

2 lbs/900 g Yukon Gold potatoes

⅔ cup/150 mL milk

⅓ cup/75 mL whipping cream

2 Tbsp/30 mL butter

1 tsp/5 mL chopped fresh thyme

3 oz/85 g Gorgonzola cheese,
   room temperature, in ½-inch/
   1-cm cubes

RED WINE SAUCE

1 Tbsp/15 mL butter

1½ shallots, quartered

1 tsp/5 mL crushed black pepper

2 cups/500 mL Pinot Noir

2 cups/500 mL brown veal stock
   (page 164)

1 Tbsp/15 mL hazelnut oil

1 sprig fresh thyme, chopped

BEEF

½ cup/125 mL mixed dried
   mushrooms (cèpes, chanterelles,
   morels)

4 pieces beef tenderloin, each
   7 oz/200 g

Drop of vegetable oil

*P*OTATOES CAN BE PREPARED in hundreds of different ways. In this recipe, I use Pemberton or Yukon Golds because they make great mashed potatoes. Instead of the Gorgonzola, you can use goat cheese, blue Danish or Stilton.

To make the mushroom powder, be sure the mushrooms are truly dry. If they are not, place them on a cookie sheet in the oven at 300°F/150°C for a couple of hours. Let them cool, then grind them in a food processor or coffee grinder. If you use a coffee grinder, clean it well or your coffee will have a strange taste the next day!

The mushroom powder flavours the meat, and the hazelnut oil in the red wine sauce complements the Gorgonzola mashed potatoes very well.

Makes 4 servings

MASHED POTATOES: Peel potatoes and cut them into quarters. Fill a saucepan with cold water and add a pinch of salt. Bring to a boil on medium heat and cook for 15 to 20 minutes, until fork-tender.

RED WINE SAUCE: Melt 1½ tsp/7.5 mL of the butter in a saucepan on medium heat. Sauté shallots for 4 minutes, until golden. Sprinkle with black pepper. Add wine and deglaze the pan. Cook until reduced to half, about 14 minutes. Add stock, then cook until reduced to half, about 20 minutes. Stir in hazelnut oil and bring to a boil. Add the thyme. Stir in the remaining butter. Season to taste with salt and pepper.

BEEF: Preheat the oven to 375°F/190°C.

Place dried mushrooms in a blender or food processor and mix until powdery. Rub mushroom powder into beef.

Heat a drop of vegetable oil in an ovenproof frying pan on medium heat and sear beef on both sides, 1 minute per side. Roast in the oven for 5 minutes (for rare, longer if you like your meat well done). Transfer beef to a warmed plate. Set aside the roasting pan.

FINISH POTATOES: Drain cooked potatoes in a colander.

Combine milk, whipping cream, butter and thyme in a saucepan on medium heat. Bring to a boil, turn down the heat to low, cook for 2 minutes, then set aside.

Place potatoes in a kitchen mixer with a paddle attachment and mix for 2 minutes. With the motor running, mix for 1 minute while slowly adding the milk mixture. With the motor still running, add cheese, one cube at a time.

FINISH SAUCE: Just before serving, deglaze the roasting pan with red wine sauce on medium heat. Turn up the heat and bring the sauce to a boil. Strain the sauce through a sieve into a warmed sauceboat.

TO SERVE: Place a beef tenderloin and some mashed potatoes on each warmed plate. Serve the red wine sauce on the side.

VEAL CUTLETS and Lobster with
Creamy Tarragon Sauce

. . . .

VEAL AND LOBSTER

4 veal cutlets, bone in, each
   12 oz/340 g

4 Tbsp/60 mL unsalted butter

2 shallots, chopped

2 live lobsters, each 2 lbs/900 g,
   or 4 lobster tails,
   each 3 to 4 oz/85 to 115 g

1 Tbsp/15 mL olive oil

1 tomato, quartered

2 Tbsp/30 mL cognac

½ cup/125 mL Chardonnay

2 cups/500 mL brown veal stock
   (page 164)

1 cup/250 mL whipping cream

1 Tbsp/15 mL chopped fresh tarragon

1 Tbsp/15 mL chopped fresh chervil

GARNISH

Drop of olive oil

1 lb/450 g fresh egg or spinach
   fettuccine

1 Tbsp/15 mL unsalted butter

1 leek, white part only, julienned

VEAL GOES VERY WELL with lobster, crayfish or crab. In general, most white meats can be paired with shellfish. Tarragon gives this dish a nice fresh flavour. If you don't have lobster, you can use prawns and finish the sauce with lobster oil instead of butter.
Makes 4 servings

VEAL AND LOBSTER: Season veal cutlets with salt and pepper. Heat a drop of olive oil in a frying pan on medium heat and sear cutlets for 5 minutes on each side, until golden. Remove veal. Add 1 tsp/15 mL of the unsalted butter and sauté shallots for 2 minutes, until translucent.

Use a large, heavy knife to cut lobsters in half lengthwise. Heat olive oil in a frying pan. Add lobster halves (or tails), shallots and tomato, and sauté for 1 minute, until lobsters begin to turn red.

Add cognac, deglaze the pan, then step back from the stove and light the cognac with a match. Let the flame die down, add wine and cook until reduced to half, about 5 minutes. Stir in stock and whipping cream and cook for 10 minutes, until liquid is reduced to a quarter.

Remove lobster from the sauce, take meat out of the tails and claws, and set aside. Put the shells back into the sauce. Turn down the heat to low and cook for 10 minutes.

Strain sauce through a sieve into a blender. Discard the shells and other solids. Mix the sauce in a blender for 1 minute. Add the remaining unsalted butter and tarragon and mix for 30 seconds.

Place the sauce in a clean saucepan. Season to taste with salt and pepper. Stir in chervil.

GARNISH: Fill a saucepan with hot salted water and bring to a boil on high heat. Add a drop of olive oil and cook the fettuccine for 2 minutes, until al dente. Stir pasta so that it cooks properly and does not stick. Drain in a colander and place fettuccine in a clean saucepan.

Melt unsalted butter in another saucepan on medium heat and sauté leek for 3 minutes, until soft and translucent. Add leeks to cooked fettuccine and mix well.

TO SERVE: Add veal and lobster to the sauce and reheat gently. On each warmed plate, arrange a veal cutlet, a quarter of the fettucine and a quarter of the lobster, then spoon 1 Tbsp/15 mL sauce over veal and lobster. Serve with extra sauce in a sauceboat on the side.

Oriental-style PORK LOIN with
Braised Daikon and Shiitake Mushrooms

. . . .

*T*HIS SIMPLE PREPARATION can be used to cook pork chops or pork bellies. In fact this spice mixture pairs well with any white meat (chicken, veal or pork). When this dish cooks, it reminds me of Hong Kong, where this smell wafts from small street-front shops late at night and early in the morning.

Makes 4 servings

Season pork loin with salt and pepper. Heat sesame oil in a large saucepan on medium heat, then sear pork loin for 5 minutes, until golden. Turn pork loin over. Add butter. Sauté carrot, onion, shallot and garlic for 3 minutes, until vegetables are golden.

Place bay leaf, cinnamon, star anise, black pepper and Szechuan pepper in a piece of cheesecloth. Remove vegetables from the saucepan using a slotted spoon and add them to the spices in the cheesecloth. Tie cheesecloth closed using butcher's string, then place in the saucepan.

Add honey and ginger. Cook for 1 minute. Pour soy sauce over pork loin, then cook for 5 minutes, until sauce boils. Add stock and turn down the heat to medium-low. Cover the saucepan with a lid and cook for 70 minutes. Add daikon and mushrooms, then cook, covered, for 10 minutes.

Use a slotted spoon to transfer pork loin and vegetables to a warmed plate. Bring stock to a boil. Remove spice mixture in cheesecloth and discard. Add chopped cilantro.

TO SERVE: Cut pork loin into ¼-inch/5-mm slices. Place slices on a warmed serving platter and arrange vegetables beside them. Sprinkle with sesame seeds and garnish with cilantro tips. Serve sauce in a sauceboat on the side.

1½ lbs/750 g boneless pork loin

1½ tsp/7.5 mL sesame oil

1 tsp/5 mL butter

1 carrot, in ½-inch/1-cm cubes

1 onion, in ½-inch/1-cm cubes

1 shallot, halved

2 cloves garlic

1 bay leaf

1 cinnamon stick

2 pieces star anise

¼ tsp/1 mL crushed black pepper

1½ tsp/7.5 mL Szechuan pepper

1 Tbsp/15 mL liquid honey

1 Tbsp/15 mL fresh ginger, peeled
   and chopped

½ cup/125 mL soy sauce

3 cups/750 mL brown veal stock
   (page 164)

1 lb/450 g daikon, in 1-inch/
   2.5-cm cubes

2 cups/500 mL fresh shiitake
   mushrooms, halved

1 Tbsp/15 mL chopped fresh cilantro

1 tsp/5 mL toasted sesame seeds
   for garnish

1 cup/250 mL cilantro leaves
   for garnish

Honey-barbecued
SHORT RIBS with Rosemary-glazed
Corn on the Cob

. . . .

BEEF

4 lbs/1.8 kg beef ribs

1 carrot, in 1-inch/2.5-cm cubes

1 onion, in 1-inch/2.5-cm cubes

1 stalk celery, in 1-inch/2.5-cm cubes

4 cloves garlic, chopped

2 bay leaves

1 Tbsp/15 mL salt

½ cup/125 mL Worcestershire sauce

½ cup/125 mL liquid honey

½ cup/125 mL soy sauce

2 Tbsp/30 mL HP sauce

1 Tbsp/15 mL tandoori paste

CORN

12 cups/3 L water

2 cups/500 mL milk

1 sprig fresh thyme, chopped

¼ tsp/1 mL salt

6 ears corn, shucked

½ cup/125 mL butter

⅓ cup/75 mL liquid honey

1 Tbsp/15 mL chopped fresh
 rosemary

*T*HE CANNERY STAFF like this dish a lot. Use this recipe to marinate any barbecued foods such as pork chops, prime rib or any roast. I like to grill or roast the ribs on low heat, so the honey in the marinade doesn't caramelize too quickly and burn. The meat retains its juice when grilled slowly, making it very tender. If you don't have a barbecue, cook the ribs in a 350°F/180°C oven for 20 minutes. Serve with slices of toasted country bread.

Makes 4 servings

BEEF: Place ribs, carrot, onion, celery, garlic and bay leaves in a saucepan. Add cold water to cover. Stir in salt and bring to a boil on medium heat. Turn down the heat to low, cover with a lid and simmer for 1 hour, until meat falls slightly from the bone. Use a slotted spoon to remove ribs and set aside until cool. (Strain the cooking liquid and discard solids, then freeze the strained liquid to make a stock or soup.)

Combine Worcestershire sauce, honey, soy sauce, HP sauce and tandoori paste in a bowl. Add beef ribs, cover and marinate overnight in the refrigerator.

CORN: Preheat the oven to 350°F/180°C. Cut six sheets of aluminum foil, 9 × 12 inches/23 × 30 cm.

Combine water, milk, thyme and salt in a stockpot on medium heat. Bring to a boil. Add corn and cook for 15 minutes, until soft.

Combine butter, honey and rosemary in a small saucepan on medium heat. Allow butter and honey to melt together, then stir to mix well.

Place one ear of corn on a sheet of foil, shiny side facing in. Pour a sixth of the melted butter mixture over corn and season to taste with salt and pepper. Fold the four corners of the foil to the centre and twist closed so you have an airtight pouch. Repeat with the remaining corn. Place wrapped corn in the oven and cook for 15 minutes, until warm.

FINISH BEEF: Remove ribs from the refrigerator half an hour before grilling. Drain ribs and save the marinade. Preheat the barbecue to low. Grill ribs for 15 to 20 minutes, occasionally brushing meat

with the reserved marinade. When ribs are crispy and glazed, turn them over and brush the other side with marinade. Continue grilling for 5 to 10 minutes, occasionally brushing meat with more marinade until ribs are golden brown, crispy and glazed.

TO SERVE: Place the ribs on a warmed serving platter. Unwrap the corn, reserving the butter sauce. Arrange the corn around the ribs. Pour the butter sauce over the corn.

WILD DUCK Duo:
Roasted Breast and Braised Legs
with Glazed Turnips

. . . .

*I*N THE FALL, we sometimes feature wild game such as deer, musk ox, venison or wild boar at the restaurant. If you like meat, wild game has a wonderful taste and is good for you. For this duck recipe, I like to cook the meat medium-rare, which is why I pan-fry the breast. However, the legs need to be braised so the meat doesn't become tough.

This is a good way to prepare wild duck, but you can use the same recipe for any wild birds, such as goose, grouse or pheasant. If wild duck is not available, you can use farm duck. In that case, shorten the cooking time by half an hour. Pierce the meat with a fork or a sharp knife to make sure it is tender.

Save any remaining cooking liquid in the freezer to use later as part of a brown stock for poultry recipes.

Makes 4 servings

DUCK: Preheat the oven to 375°F/190°C. Use a boning knife to cut off duck legs, thighs and breasts. Set aside duck breasts. Use a heavy chopping knife to cut duck carcass into six pieces, each 1½-inch/3-cm thick, and place in a roasting pan with the duck legs and thighs, carrot, onion, celery and shallots. Add a drop of vegetable oil. Roast in the oven for 20 minutes, until golden. Add tomato paste, toss gently and cook for 5 minutes. Transfer to a saucepan on medium heat. Add wine to the roasting pan in which you cooked the duck and deglaze. Pour into the saucepan over the duck. Add thyme, black pepper and stock. Turn down the heat to low and cook for 90 minutes, until meat is soft. Remove from the heat and reserve.

TURNIPS: Combine turnips, water, honey, butter, thyme and salt in a saucepan on medium heat. Cover with a lid and cook for about 20 minutes, until turnips are completely dry.

Take off the lid and add ¼ cup/60 mL of the cooking liquid from the duck. Continue cooking for about 5 minutes, until turnips are golden. Sprinkle with parsley.

continued overleaf >

DUCK

2 small wild ducks (mallard, wood, pintail), each 25 oz/700 g

1 carrot, in 1-inch/2.5-cm cubes

1 small onion, in 1-inch/2.5-cm cubes

1 stalk celery, in 1-inch/2.5-cm cubes

2 shallots, sliced

Drop of vegetable oil

2 tsp/10 mL tomato paste

2 cups/500 mL Chardonnay

2 sprigs fresh thyme, chopped

1 tsp/5 mL crushed black pepper

3 cups/750 mL brown chicken stock (page 164)

¼ cup/60 mL cognac

1 tsp/5 mL butter

TURNIPS

1 lb/450 g turnips, quartered

1 cup/250 mL water

1 tsp/5 mL liquid honey

1 Tbsp/15 mL butter

1 sprig fresh thyme, chopped

¼ tsp/1 mL salt

1 tsp/5 mL chopped fresh Italian flat-leaf parsley

FINISH DUCK: Preheat the oven to 375°F/190°C. Season duck breasts on both sides with salt and black pepper. Add a drop of vegetable oil to an ovenproof frying pan on medium heat and sear duck breasts for 2 minutes on each side. Place the frying pan in the oven and roast for 5 minutes, until duck skin is crispy. Remove the frying pan from the oven and set it aside.

Remove the duck legs and thighs from the stock, reserving the stock, and place them with the breasts in the oven to warm up, about 5 minutes. Transfer the duck to a warmed plate and let rest for 5 minutes.

While the duck is resting, make the sauce. Add cognac to the frying pan and deglaze. Add 1½ cups/375 mL of the cooking liquid from the saucepan. Cook until reduced to half, about 10 minutes, then stir in butter and season to taste with salt and pepper.

TO SERVE: Slice and arrange duck breasts, legs and thighs (discard the duck carcass pieces) on a warmed serving platter. Place turnips on the side and serve the sauce in a warmed sauceboat.

Orange Zest and RABBIT LEGS Confit with Roasted Balsamic and Port Figs

. . . .

CONFIT IS A COOKING PROCESS that involves slow cooking in a simmering liquid, often a fat or an oil. You can make a confit with pork or duck fat, but I prefer olive oil, which has a more delicate flavour. For this confit, rabbit legs work better than other parts. You can buy them at a butcher shop, but if you have a whole rabbit, use the legs and save the rest to make a sauté. Strain the oil from the confit through a sieve into a clean container and freeze until the next time you make this dish. It will keep frozen for up to 2 months.

Makes 4 servings

RABBIT: Combine rock salt, thyme, rosemary, garlic, bay leaves and black pepper in a bowl. Rub mixture into rabbit legs. Place in a covered pan and marinate in the refrigerator for 2 hours.

Place rabbit in a colander and rinse under cold running water to remove excess salt. Save the rosemary and thyme. Drain rabbit on paper towels.

Combine the reserved thyme and rosemary, olive oil, sherry and orange zest in a saucepan. Add rabbit legs and cook on medium heat for about 7 minutes, until oil starts to simmer. Turn down the heat to low and cook for 1 hour, until rabbit is cooked. Prick the rabbit with a bamboo skewer to check if it is done (the meat should be soft). Use a slotted spoon to gently remove meat from the oil and drain on paper towels.

FIGS: Melt butter in a saucepan on medium heat. Sauté shallots and bacon for 2 minutes, until translucent. Stir in balsamic vinegar and cook until reduced to a third, about 15 minutes. Stir in port and cook until reduced to half, about 10 minutes.

Turn down the heat to low. Add figs and cook for 10 minutes, until they puff up a little bit. Do not overcook or cook too quickly, or figs will split open. Sprinkle with black pepper.

SALAD: Place arugula, mesclun and chervil in a salad bowl and toss with pistachio oil, vegetable oil and sherry vinegar. Season to taste with salt and pepper.

TO SERVE: Arrange rabbit legs, figs and the shallot-bacon mixture on a warmed serving platter. Garnish with thyme and rosemary.

RABBIT

½ cup/125 mL rock salt

2 sprigs fresh thyme

½ sprig fresh rosemary

6 cloves garlic, crushed

2 bay leaves

1 tsp/5 mL crushed black pepper

4 rabbit legs, back legs only
   (about 2 lbs/900 g)

8 cups/2 L olive oil

1 Tbsp/15 mL sherry

1 orange, zest of

FIGS

1 tsp/5 mL butter

1 cup/250 mL quartered shallots

8 oz/225 g bacon, in ½-inch/
   1-cm cubes

1 cup/250 mL balsamic vinegar

½ cup/125 mL ruby port

1 lb/450 g Black Mission
   (or Turkish) figs

½ tsp/2.5 mL crushed black pepper

SALAD

2 oz/60 g arugula
   (about 2 cups/500 mL)

3 oz/85 g mesclun
   (about 3 cups/750 mL)

½ cup/125 mL fresh chervil

2 Tbsp/30 mL pistachio oil or truffle
   oil or vegetable oil

1 Tbsp/15 mL vegetable oil

2 Tbsp/30 mL sherry vinegar

1 sprig fresh thyme for garnish

½ sprig fresh rosemary for garnish

Creamy Chinese Artichoke RISOTTO
with Black Truffle

· · · · · · · · · · ·

1 cup/250 mL rock salt

10 oz/285 g Chinese artichokes
   (crosnes)

1 black truffle or 2 Tbsp/30 mL
   wild mushrooms

2 Tbsp/30 mL butter

1 Tbsp/15 mL olive oil

6 shallots, chopped

2 cups/500 mL arborio rice

1½ cups/375 mL Sauvignon Blanc

1 bouquet garni (page 15)

3 cups/750 mL vegetable stock
   (page 163)

1½ cups/375 mL whipping cream

1 tsp/5 mL chopped Italian parsley

2 Tbsp/30 mL freshly grated
   Parmesan cheese

4 sprigs chervil for garnish

CHINESE ARTICHOKES are known as crosnes in Europe, where they were first introduced from Asia and where they became very popular in the nineteenth century. These root vegetables, which have a taste similar to that of regular globe artichokes, pair very well with truffles.

If you can't find Chinese artichokes at the market, you can substitute fresh globe artichokes, Jerusalem artichokes, cardoons or black salsify.

Makes 4 servings

Fill a saucepan with water, stir in 1 Tbsp/15 mL of the rock salt and bring to a boil on high heat.

While the water is heating up, place the artichokes in a bowl with the remaining rock salt and mix well with your hands for 5 minutes in order to peel the skin. Discard the salt and rinse artichokes under cold running water until the water is completely clean. Place artichokes in the boiling water and cook for about 4 minutes, until al dente. Transfer to a colander and cool under cold running water.

Thinly slice truffle using a Japanese or truffle mandoline. Chop half of the slices into small cubes and set the other half aside.

Melt butter and olive oil in a saucepan on medium heat. Sauté shallots, the cubed truffle and Chinese artichokes for 2 minutes, until shallots become translucent, all the while stirring with a spatula. Add rice and stir for 2 minutes. Add wine and bouquet garni and, stirring frequently, cook until reduced to half, about 5 minutes. Stir in half of the stock and a good pinch of salt. Turn down the heat to medium-low. Add whipping cream and the rest of the stock and, stirring frequently, cook for 10 minutes. By now, the rice should be almost done. Season to taste with salt and pepper, stirring constantly so risotto does not stick. Discard the bouquet garni and add the parsley.

TO SERVE: Transfer risotto to a warmed serving platter. Sprinkle with Parmesan cheese and the sliced truffle. Garnish with chervil.

MUNG BEANS with
Curry Oil–roasted Tofu

. . . .

*I*NDIAN CUISINE offers many delicious vegetarian options, and East Indian markets are full of interesting grains and beans with which to make these dishes.

Makes 4 servings

CURRY OIL: Place curry paste and olive oil in a blender and mix for 2 minutes. Transfer to a bowl, cover and allow to infuse overnight in the refrigerator.

The oil and paste should have separated. Carefully pour the infused oil into a clean bowl and discard the remaining paste. Cover and refrigerate until needed, up to 1 month.

MUNG BEANS AND TOFU: Place mung beans in a bowl, cover with cold water and leave to soak overnight at room temperature. Drain beans and rinse under cold running water.

Heat olive oil in a saucepan on medium heat and sauté carrot, celery, shallots and garlic for 1 minute, until translucent. Stir in turmeric, saffron, ground cumin, tomato paste and curry powder. Cook for 1 minute. Turn up the heat to high. Add drained mung beans and stock, season to taste with salt and pepper, and cook for 12 minutes, until beans are soft.

Season tofu with salt and pepper. Heat 1 Tbsp/15 mL of the curry oil in a nonstick frying pan on high heat. Sauté tofu for 5 minutes, stirring, until golden.

GARNISH: Cut pappadams in half. Turn on the oven grill. Heat half a pappadam under the grill for about 10 seconds, until it becomes soft. Roll it into a cone shape, then allow to cool and harden for 10 seconds. Repeat with the remaining half pappadams.

TO SERVE: Place beans on a warmed serving platter and arrange tofu on top.

Place cilantro in a salad bowl, add the remaining curry oil and toss together. Place dressed cilantro into the pappadum cones. Arrange the cones on the side of the platter.

CURRY OIL

1 Tbsp/15 mL curry paste

¼ cup/60 mL olive oil

MUNG BEANS AND TOFU

1½ cups/375 mL mung beans

1 Tbsp/15 mL olive oil

1 carrot, in ¼-inch/5-mm cubes

1 stalk celery, in ¼-inch/5-mm cubes

2 shallots, chopped

1 tsp/5 mL chopped garlic

½ tsp/2.5 mL turmeric

Pinch of saffron

Pinch of toasted ground cumin
   (page 91)

1 Tbsp/15 mL tomato paste

½ tsp/2.5 mL curry powder

3 cups/750 mL vegetable stock
   (page 163)

8 oz/225 g firm tofu, in ½-inch/
   1-cm cubes

GARNISH

2 pappadams

1 cup fresh cilantro leaves

Sautéed Mediterranean VEGETABLES
in a Crispy Parmesan Cup
. . . .

PARMESAN CUPS

2 cups/500 mL coarsely grated
Parmesan cheese

2 sun-dried tomatoes, finely chopped

1 Tbsp/15 mL chopped fresh thyme

VEGETABLES

2 Tbsp/30 mL extra-virgin olive oil

1 zucchini, in ½-inch/1-cm cubes

1 red bell pepper, in ½-inch/
1-cm cubes

1 green bell pepper, in ½-inch/
1-cm cubes

1 yellow bell pepper, in ½-inch/
1-cm cubes

1 eggplant, in ½-inch/1-cm cubes

1 red onion, in ½-inch/1-cm cubes

4 Roma tomatoes, chopped

2 Tbsp/30 mL drained capers

¼ cup/60 mL basil and olive oil
vinaigrette (page 165)

2 Tbsp/30 mL chopped fresh basil
for garnish

*T*HIS IS A VERY TASTY vegetarian main dish. To make the Parmesan cups, buy Parmesan cheese in a block and shred it at home with a cheese grater. Prepackaged shredded cheese will dry out faster. You can use cheddar cheese instead of the Parmesan. Garnish the vegetables with a little pesto (page 58).

Makes 4 servings

PARMESAN CUPS: Preheat the oven to 375°F/190°C. Line a cookie sheet with parchment paper.

Combine Parmesan, sun-dried tomatoes and thyme in a bowl. Divide the Parmesan mixture into 4 mounds on the parchment paper and shape them into 4 rounds, each 4 inches/10 cm in diameter. Bake in the oven for 6 minutes, until light golden.

Remove from the oven and allow to cool for 10 seconds. While still warm, place each Parmesan round over an upside-down cup to form it into a cup shape. Allow them to cool until they harden.

VEGETABLES: Heat 1 tsp/5 mL of the olive oil in a frying pan on high heat. Cook zucchini for 2 minutes, until soft, and set aside. Repeat the process separately for bell peppers, eggplant, red onion and tomatoes, and set aside.

TO SERVE: Place a Parmesan cup on each serving plate.

Combine all the sautéed vegetables and capers in a large saucepan with basil vinaigrette. Reheat them on medium heat. Mix well and divide among the Parmesan cups. Garnish with basil.

DESSERTS

. . . .

A DESSERT SHOULD BE LIGHT,

small and simple—and a memorable end to the meal.

Finish each plate with ice cream, crème fraîche or coulis

for a nice contrast, but use only a small amount

so that you don't overpower the dessert.

At home, I like to serve dessert in a different room,

by the fireplace with a glass of port, Champagne or

one of British Columbia's excellent icewines.

White CHOCOLATE and Fig
Mousse Mille-feuilles

. . . .

MOUSSE

3½ oz/100 g dried Black Mission figs

1¼ cups/360 mL whipping cream

6 oz/170 g white chocolate, finely
    chopped

3 leaves gelatin

1 cup/250 mL mascarpone cheese

3 egg yolks

2 Tbsp/30 mL Grand Marnier or
    other orange liqueur

PASTRY

7 oz/200 g frozen puff pastry, thawed

1 orange, zest of

½ tsp/2.5 mL anise seeds

1 egg yolk

1 tsp/2.5 mL icing sugar

I LOVE DRIED FRUIT, especially figs. This mousse filling is very versatile: you can use it to stuff dates or apricots, or you can add dried fruit and pistachios to it before filling Sicilian cannelloni. To save time, make the mousse filling a day ahead. Serve the mille-feuilles with chocolate sauce (page 168) and a glass of port.

Makes 4 to 6 servings

MOUSSE: Place dried figs in a bowl, fill it to the top with water, cover and allow to soak overnight at room temperature. Remove and discard the stems. Cut figs into ¼-inch/5-mm cubes.

Place whipping cream in a kitchen mixer with a whisk attachment, and whip until it forms soft peaks. Transfer to a bowl, cover and refrigerate until needed.

Melt white chocolate in a stainless steel bowl over a saucepan of hot water on medium heat, stirring constantly. Keep chocolate at 100°F/40°C until needed.

Place gelatin and cold water in a bowl and allow to soak for 5 minutes, until soft. Remove soaked gelatin leaves from water and squeeze gently to remove excess water. Place softened gelatin in another stainless steel bowl over a saucepan of hot water on medium heat. Stir until gelatin melts.

Place mascarpone cheese in a clean bowl and beat in egg yolks. Place 2 Tbsp/30 mL of the mascarpone mixture in another bowl, add half of the melted gelatin and mix well. Add the remaining gelatin and mix well. Add the remaining mascarpone mixture and mix well. Slowly add the melted chocolate and fold in gently using a rubber spatula. Fold in diced figs, whipped cream and Grand Marnier. Cover and refrigerate for 5 hours before serving. This mousse will keep refrigerated for up to 4 days.

PASTRY: Roll out puff pastry on a lightly floured surface until
⅛ inch/3 mm thick. Cut dough into a 16-inch/40-cm square. Sprinkle
with orange zest and anise seeds.

Use a knife to cut 4 to 6 strips, each 4 × 2 inches/10 × 5 cm. Wrap
the strips in plastic wrap, then put them in the freezer for 2 hours.

Preheat the oven to 350°F/180°C. Line a cookie sheet with
parchment paper.

Place frozen dough strips on the parchment paper, brush with
egg yolk and bake in the oven for 20 minutes, until puffy and golden.
Sprinkle with icing sugar and bake for 5 minutes, until the tops are
nicely glazed. Remove the strips from the oven and place them on a
wire rack to cool.

Cut each strip in half lengthwise to make a top and bottom. Place
fig mousse on half of the strips and cover with the remaining strips.

TO SERVE: Place the mille-feuilles on individual plates.

Summer BERRY Terrine

. . . .

*T*HIS SUMMER RECIPE is a big success at the restaurant. It is very important to use ripe fruit. You can also use seasonal fruit like mango, pear, orange or pineapple. I don't recommend using kiwi because it is too acid and the gelatin will not set properly.

If you omit the liquor from the citrus coulis, you can easily place it in a ramekin or plastic container for your child's lunch box.

Makes 10 servings

BASE: Place gelatin leaves in a bowl with cold water and cover. Allow to soak for 5 minutes, until soft.

Combine sugar and water in a saucepan on medium heat and bring to a boil. Add strawberries, raspberries and blackberries, then cook for 2 minutes, until soft. Remove from the heat and allow to cool for 2 minutes. Place in a blender and mix for 20 seconds. Strain through a sieve into a clean bowl and discard seeds.

Remove soaked gelatin leaves from water and squeeze gently to remove excess water. Stir gelatin into the warm base mixture and let sit for 15 minutes at room temperature.

FILLING: Line a terrine pan 8 × 3½ inches/20 × 7½ cm with plastic wrap. Make sure to smooth it well along the edges.

Place rinsed strawberries, raspberries, blackberries and blueberries on paper towels to dry. Mix fruit gently in a small bowl, sprinkle with chopped mint and transfer to the terrine pan. Gently pour the base mixture over the top and allow to set in the refrigerator for 4 hours.

TO SERVE: Place the terrine pan upside down on a cutting board. Tug gently on the plastic wrap to release the terrine from the pan. Use a thin knife blade warmed in hot water to cut slices ¾ inch/ 2 cm thick. Serve on individual plates with a spoonful of citrus coulis or orange sorbet. Garnish with mint leaves, fresh berries and flower petals.

BASE

8 leaves gelatin

½ cup/250 mL sugar

2 cups/500 mL water

2 oz/60 g strawberries, destemmed
    (about ½ cup/125 mL)

2 oz/60 g raspberries
    (about ½ cup/125 mL)

2 oz/60 g blackberries
    (about ½ cup/125 mL)

FILLING

6 oz/170 g strawberries, destemmed
    (about 1½ cups/375 mL)

6 oz/170 g raspberries
    (about 2 cups/500 mL)

6 oz/170 g blackberries
    (about 2 cups/500 mL)

6 oz/170 g blueberries
    (about 2 cups/500 mL)

2 Tbsp/30 mL chopped fresh mint

Citrus coulis (page 167) or
    orange sorbet for garnish

Fresh mint leaves for garnish

4 or 5 fresh berries for garnish

4 or 5 flower petals for garnish

Thai MANGO Clafoutis

. . . .

½ vanilla bean or ½ tsp/2.5 mL
vanilla extract

½ cup/125 mL milk

½ cup/125 mL whipping cream

⅓ cup/75 mL melted unsalted butter
+ 1 Tbsp/15 mL for the tart pan

1 cup/250 mL all-purpose flour
+ 1 tsp/5 mL for the tart pan

½ cup/125 mL sugar

1 tsp/5 mL baking powder

Pinch of salt

3 eggs

3 mangoes

1 tsp/5 mL icing sugar

8 scoops butterscotch ice cream
for garnish

*T*HIS RUSTIC DESSERT from France could also be served at an afternoon tea. Traditionally, clafoutis is made with cherries. The fruit is washed, the stems removed and the whole cherries cooked in a crêpelike batter without removing the pits.

We make this variation using Thai or Indian mangoes, which are available from March to August. They are a very sweet, green-yellow fruit with a rich, silky texture and a flavour that hints of pine and peach. You could also make this dessert with berries, apples or bananas. Just like cheesecake, when cooked, turn off the oven and let the clafoutis cool with the oven door partly open.

Makes 8 servings

Preheat the oven to 350°F/180°C.

Cut vanilla bean in half lengthwise and scrape out seeds. Combine vanilla bean husk and seeds, milk and whipping cream in a saucepan on medium heat and bring to a boil. Cover with a lid and remove from heat. Let it infuse as it cools for half an hour. Remove and discard vanilla bean husk.

Brush the 1 Tbsp/15 mL of melted butter inside a 10-inch/25-cm ceramic tart pan and sprinkle with the 1 tsp/5 mL of flour to make sure the cake will not stick.

Place the remaining flour, sugar, baking powder and salt in a bowl and make a hole in the middle. Place eggs in the hole and mix slowly with a whisk. While whisking, slowly add the milk mixture. Mix well until there are no lumps. Stir in the remaining melted butter.

Peel and core mango, then cut each into 10 equal wedges. Arrange mango wedges in the bottom of the tart pan and gently pour the custard over them. Bake in the oven for about 35 minutes, until custard has set. Sprinkle with icing sugar and bake for 5 minutes. Turn off the oven and leave the tart inside with the door partly open to cool down. Serve at room temperature.

TO SERVE: Slice the clafoutis into 8 portions. Spoon portions onto individual plates and serve each with a scoop of butterscotch ice cream.

Baked APPLES with
Toasted Pistachio Crème Fraîche

. . . .

BAKED APPLES are a traditional autumn recipe because so many varieties are available at that time of year. In this recipe, you can use any firm, sweet, juicy apple, such as Royal Gala, Spartan, Fuji, Ambrosia or McIntosh.

If you like, stuff the apples with a mixture of cinnamon, raisins and nuts before baking. Then serve the apples warm from the oven with crème fraîche, vanilla ice cream or a plate of shortbread cookies.

Makes 4 servings

CRÈME FRAÎCHE: Combine whipping cream and buttermilk in a bowl. Cover and leave at room temperature for 30 hours. The cream will thicken.

Preheat the oven to 375°F/190°C. Place pistachios on a cookie sheet and roast in the oven for about 15 minutes, stirring them every 4 minutes, until very light blond. Remove from oven and cool. Combine pistachio nuts and sugar in a bowl. Set aside.

APPLES: Preheat the oven to 350°F/180°C. Remove apple centres with an apple corer. Discard cores and place apples on an ovenproof tray greased with 1½ tsp/7.5 mL of the butter.

Combine brown sugar, honey, lemon juice, Calvados and the remaining butter in a saucepan on low heat and cook for 5 minutes. Pour over apples and bake in the oven for 35 minutes, basting frequently, until apples soften.

TO SERVE: Place a baked apple on each warmed serving plate. Pour cooking liquid over apples and serve with crème fraîche in a bowl on the side.

CRÈME FRAÎCHE

1½ cups/375 mL whipping cream

2 Tbsp/30 mL buttermilk

⅔ cup/150 mL peeled and chopped pistachio nuts

3 Tbsp/45 mL sugar

APPLES

4 apples, unpeeled

2 Tbsp/30 mL butter

⅓ cup/75 mL brown sugar

½ cup/125 mL liquid honey

½ lemon, juice of

3 Tbsp/45 mL Calvados or cognac or Armagnac

Dark Chocolate BROWNIES
with Roasted Nuts

. . . .

⅓ cup/75 mL walnuts

⅓ cup/75 mL hazelnuts

⅓ cup/75 mL almonds

1 Tbsp/15 mL butter, melted

2 Tbsp/30 mL all-purpose flour

8 oz/225 g unsalted butter, in
   ½-inch/1-cm cubes, room
   temperature

8 oz/225 g dark chocolate,
   finely chopped

5 egg yolks, room temperature

5 egg whites, room temperature

Pinch of salt

½ cup/125 mL brown sugar

1 Tbsp/15 mL liquid honey

¼ cup/60 mL raspberry coulis
   (page 167)

I LIKE TO MAKE BROWNIES with butter instead of shortening because they taste richer. To bring out the flavour of the nuts, roast them first. It will also make them crunchier and complement the chocolate very well. Serve these decadent brownies at the end of a meal with vanilla ice cream or as a snack with afternoon tea.

Makes 8 servings

Preheat the oven to 375°F/190°C. Spread walnuts, hazelnuts and almonds on a cookie sheet and roast for about 7 minutes, stirring occasionally, until golden. Remove from the oven and allow to cool.

Turn down the oven to 350°F/180°C. Brush a 10-inch/25-cm springform pan with melted butter and sprinkle with 1 Tbsp/15 mL of the flour. Turn the pan upside down and shake gently to remove excess flour.

Place roasted nuts on a cutting board and use a rolling pin to crush them into small pieces.

Melt unsalted butter and chocolate in a stainless steel bowl over a saucepan of hot water on medium heat, stirring constantly. Remove from the heat and allow to cool for 2 minutes. Slowly whisk in egg yolks, one at a time, mixing well before adding the next.

In a kitchen mixer, whisk egg whites in a separate bowl with a pinch of salt, until doubled in volume and firm. While mixing for 2 minutes, slowly add brown sugar and honey.

Use a wooden spoon to mix egg whites into chocolate mix. Add roasted nuts and the remaining flour, and mix well. Pour batter into the baking pan and bake for 20 minutes, until brownies have risen. Very carefully remove from the oven in one piece and allow to cool.

TO SERVE: Place the brownie on a large serving plate. Slice into individual portions and drizzle each with raspberry coulis.

APRICOT Tart
with Hazelnut Crust

· · · · · · · · · ·

PASTRY

8 oz/225 g butter
   (about 1 cup/250 mL)
1 egg
2 Tbsp/30 mL water
½ cup/125 mL brown sugar
1½ cups/375 mL chopped roasted
   hazelnuts
3 cups/750 mL all-purpose flour
1 Tbsp/15 mL butter, melted

FILLING

1 Tbsp/15 mL butter
¼ cup/60 mL sugar
2 lbs/900 g apricots, halved
   and pitted
1 cup/250 mL whipping cream
4 eggs
¼ cup/60 mL milk

THIS DESSERT IS A VERY NICE END to a summer meal because it is moist and fragrant. Although you can make this tart with pears, apples, peaches or figs, Okanagan apricots work well in this recipe, so make it in August when the apricots are at their peak. It is important to use really ripe apricots for the filling and a slightly firm one for the garnish. Serve this tart with an Okanagan icewine or another dessert wine.

Makes 8 servings

PASTRY: Place the 8 oz/225 g butter, egg, water and brown sugar in a kitchen mixer with a paddle attachment and mix for 2 minutes, until smooth. Add hazelnuts and mix for 20 seconds. Add flour and mix for 15 seconds, until dough becomes firm. Be careful not to overmix. Wrap the dough in plastic wrap and refrigerate for 5 hours. (You could make the recipe up to this point a few days in advance and keep in the refrigerator for up to 5 days.) Take the dough out of the refrigerator and let it sit at room temperature for 30 minutes before using.

Preheat the oven to 375°F/190°C. Brush an 8-inch/20-cm spring-form tart pan with melted butter.

Place the dough on a lightly floured cutting board and sprinkle it with a little flour. Roll out the dough to a rough circle about 10 inches/25 cm in diameter and ⅛ inch/3 mm thick. Line the tart pan with the dough, trim off any extra and use a fork to score all around the edge of the tart. Place the tart pan on a cookie sheet.

FILLING: Melt butter in a saucepan on low to medium heat and stir in 1 Tbsp/15 mL of the sugar. Add half of the apricots and cook for 5 minutes, then turn down the heat to low. Stir in ¼ cup/60 mL of the whipping cream and cook for 15 minutes, until the apricots are soft. Transfer the apricot mixture to a bowl and allow it to cool.

In a bowl, mix together eggs, milk, the remaining whipping cream and 2 Tbsp/30 mL of the sugar for 1 minute. Add the cooled apricot mixture and mix well. Arrange the remaining apricot halves on the bottom of the tart shell and gently pour the cooked apricot mixture over them. Bake in the oven for 10 minutes. Turn down the temperature to 325°F/160°C and bake for 20 minutes, until filling is soft set. Sprinkle 1 Tbsp/15 mL of the sugar over the tart and bake for 5 minutes. Remove the tart from the oven and allow to cool for 2 hours before serving.

TO SERVE: Unmould the tart and place it on a large serving platter. Cut individual slices and serve at room temperature.

Bartlett PEAR and
Toasted Almond Tart

. . . .

*F*OR THIS RECIPE it is important to use firm pears and poach them first. You can also use canned fruit in syrup; however, drain the fruit the day before to remove any excess syrup.

This dessert can be made with pineapple, peaches or apples. Warm chocolate sauce (page 168) and vanilla ice cream are a nice complement to this tart.

Makes 8 servings

PEARS: Combine sugar and water in a saucepan. Bring to a boil with vanilla bean, stirring constantly, and cook for 3 minutes. Turn down the heat to low. Peel the pears and place them in the syrup. Cook for 5 minutes at a gentle simmer, then turn off the heat and let the pears cool in the syrup.

PASTRY: Place flour, salt and butter in a kitchen mixer with a hook attachment and mix for 5 minutes. Add egg and milk and mix until dough forms a ball.

Remove dough from the mixer and wrap it in plastic wrap. Refrigerate and let sit for 5 hours.

Use a rolling pin to roll out dough on a lightly floured surface. Line the tart pan with the dough. Trim off the edges and prick the bottom with a fork. Refrigerate until needed, up to 12 hours.

FILLING: Place unsalted butter and sugar in a kitchen mixer with a whisk attachment and mix until fluffy. Add egg, almonds, rum and flour and mix for 3 minutes.

ASSEMBLY: Preheat the oven to 350°F/180°C. Transfer filling to the tart shell. Cut pears into thin slices and arrange on top of the filling. Bake in the oven for about 35 minutes, until the top turns golden. Take the tart out of the oven and let it set for 1 hour before serving.

TO SERVE: Serve the tart whole on a large round serving plate or cut it into 8 portions and serve each on an individual plate.

PEARS

2 cups/500 mL sugar

2 cups/500 mL water

½ vanilla bean, halved lengthwise

4 Bartlett or William pears

PASTRY

2 cups/250 mL all-purpose flour

Pinch of salt

6 oz/170 g unsalted butter,
    room temperature,
    in ½-inch/1-cm cubes

1 egg

1 Tbsp/15 mL milk

FILLING

5 oz/140 g unsalted butter

½ cup/125 mL sugar

1 egg

1 cup/250 mL chopped
    toasted almonds

1 Tbsp/15 mL dark rum

1 Tbsp/15 mL all-purpose flour

STRAWBERRIES with Fresh Mint and White Balsamic Reduction

. . . .

1½ cups/375 mL white balsamic
   vinegar or regular balsamic
   vinegar
½ cup/125 mL sugar
½ cup/125 mL water
1 lb/450 g strawberries
1 Tbsp/15 mL chopped fresh mint
4 scoops vanilla ice cream

STRAWBERRIES ARE EXCELLENT in the nearby Fraser Valley, and in my garden too! It may seem odd to use vinegar in a dessert, but white balsamic will have the consistency of molasses when reduced. If you reduce the vinegar too much and it looks like caramel, add water.

Serve these strawberries in a bowl with a scoop of vanilla ice cream. The smooth ice cream makes a nice contrast to the slight acidity of the strawberries, and the balsamic vinegar brings out the flavour of the fruit. The mint adds a refreshing taste.

Makes 4 servings

Combine balsamic vinegar, sugar and water in a saucepan on medium heat. Cook until the mixture is reduced to one third and becomes the consistency of light molasses, about 10 minutes. Transfer to a bowl and allow to cool.

Rinse strawberries in cold water. Remove and discard stems, then drain on paper towels. If strawberries are large, cut them in half. Add strawberries and mint to the cold vinegar mixture and mix well.

TO SERVE: Spoon into 4 individual bowls and serve each with a scoop of ice cream.

Pineapple and
Lemon CHEESECAKE

. . . .

CHEESECAKE IS THE MOST POPULAR and best-known dessert in Canada. There are many different recipes and several ways to make it. Use this basic recipe to invent your own versions: for example, garnish the cake with blue cheese and roasted caramelized pear, pecan and rum, or chocolate marble. It is important to let the cheesecake cool down in the oven with the door partly open. This will prevent it from cracking. For an extra touch, serve it with an apricot or mango coulis on the side.

Makes 1 cake, diameter 10 inches/25 cm

CRUST: Preheat the oven to 375°F/190°C. Place flour and sugar in a kitchen mixer with a paddle attachment and mix for 1 minute. Add unsalted butter and egg yolk, then mix for 2 minutes. Line the bottom of a 10-inch/25 cm springform pan with the pastry, pressing down lightly with your hands to make it firm. Bake in the oven for 15 minutes, until golden.

FILLING: Turn down the oven to 300°F/150°C. Peel and cut pineapple in half lengthwise. Remove and discard the hard core. Cut pineapple into ½-inch/1-cm cubes.

Melt unsalted butter in a frying pan on medium heat. Add pineapple and half of the sugar, then cook for 5 minutes, stirring constantly, until golden. Transfer to a bowl and allow to cool.

Combine cream cheese, sour cream and the remaining sugar in a kitchen mixer with a paddle attachment and beat for 5 minutes. Add whipping cream, eggs and egg yolks, one at a time, mixing well after each addition. Mix for 2 minutes. Gently stir in cooled pineapple, lemon juice and lemon zest.

Pour filling over the crust in the springform pan and bake in the oven for 90 minutes, until set. Turn off the oven and leave the cheesecake inside with the door just open to cool down for 1 hour. Remove from the oven and allow to cool for 3 hours. Refrigerate for 3 hours before serving.

TO SERVE: Warm the blade of a knife under hot running water, then use it to cut all around the edge of the cheesecake. Unmould the cheesecake and transfer it to a large serving platter. Cut the cheesecake into 12 or 14 equal parts.

CRUST

1 cup/250 mL all-purpose flour

½ cup/125 mL sugar

2 Tbsp/30 mL unsalted butter

1 egg yolk

FILLING

2 lbs/900 g pineapple

1 Tbsp/15 mL unsalted butter

⅔ cup/150 mL sugar

3 cups/750 mL cream cheese

½ cup/125 mL sour cream

1 cup/250 mL whipping cream

2 eggs

2 egg yolks

⅓ cup/75 mL lemon juice

1 lemon, zest of

Blood ᴏʀᴀɴɢ Crème Brûlée

. . . .

1 blood orange

¼ cup/60 mL sugar

6 egg yolks

½ cup/125 mL sugar

½ cup/125 mL milk

1½ cups/375 mL whipping cream

1 Tbsp/15 mL sugar

1 Tbsp/15 mL brown sugar

*T*HERE ARE MANY different flavours of crème brûlée. My favourite is orange. You can use any other citrus fruit in this recipe, but small-to-medium-sized sweet blood oranges have a nice ruby red colour and a rich citrus flavour with a raspberry aftertaste. Well known in Europe and brought to North America by Italian and Spanish immigrants, blood oranges appear in markets between December and March.

The sugar used to be caramelized by setting a red-hot iron disk with a wooden handle 1 inch/2.5 cm over the top. Nowadays, you can caramelize the sugar in the oven with a broiler element or you can buy a small blowtorch for this purpose in a specialty cookware store. Do not place the flame too close to the sugar, or it will burn before caramelizing, giving it a bitter and unpleasant taste.

Makes 4 servings

Scrub orange well under cold running water and dry with a paper towel. Use a vegetable peeler to peel orange and save the peel. Use a knife to cut orange into segments and remove the membrane, saving any juice in a bowl. Reserve the orange segments. Squeeze he remaining juice out of the membrane and add to the rest of the juice. Cut orange peel into julienne.

Combine juice and sugar in a saucepan on medium heat and bring to a boil. Turn down the heat to low, add peel and cook for 3 minutes, until soft cooked. Drain peel on paper towels.

Preheat the oven to 325°F/160°C.

Place egg yolks and sugar in a bowl and whisk together for 2 minutes, until pale in colour. Slowly add milk and whipping cream, whisking constantly. Add peel and mix well, then allow to sit and infuse for 15 minutes. Pour into ramekins 2½ inches/6 cm in diameter.

Divide orange segments among ramekins and fill with crème brûlée. Place ramekins in a baking pan and add water so that it reaches halfway up the sides of the dishes. Place the pan in the oven and bake for 60 minutes, until soft set. Remove from the oven, take the ramekins out of the pan of water and allow to cool down to room temperature. Refrigerate for 2 hours before serving.

Turn on the oven broiler to high heat. Mix together white and brown sugar in a cup. Sprinkle combined sugar evenly on top of each ramekin and place under the broiler, rotating the brûlées until sugar caramelizes and turns golden, about 1 minute.

TO SERVE: Serve the individual crème brûlées in their ramekins immediately.

Roasted FIGS in Port with
Lavender and Honey Ice Cream

. . . .

I USE FRESH BLACK MISSION FIGS in this recipe. Look for them at the market—their skin is purple-black and they are smaller than the larger, greener Turkish figs. It is important to cook the figs very slowly otherwise they will break.

If you don't have an ice cream machine, make frozen parfait (page 152) without the caramelized nuts or use store-bought vanilla ice cream. Or, serve the figs with blue cheese instead of ice cream.

Makes 4 servings

ICE CREAM: Combine milk, whipping cream, honey and lavender in a saucepan on medium heat. Bring to a boil, then cover with a lid, turn off the heat and leave on the stove for 30 minutes to infuse. Strain the mixture through a sieve and discard solids.

Place egg yolks and sugar in a bowl and whisk for 2 minutes, until yolks become pale in colour. While whisking gently, slowly pour in the milk mixture.

Transfer to a saucepan on medium heat and cook for 5 minutes, stirring with a wooden spatula, until the liquid becomes slightly thick. Do not let it boil.

Transfer to a clean bowl and place over a bowl filled with ice and water to stop the cooking. Keep stirring with the spatula to help the mixture cool down.

When the mixture is cold, transfer it to an ice cream machine and process according to the manufacturer's instructions. The ice cream will keep for up to 1 day.

FIGS: Combine brown sugar, port and water in a saucepan on medium heat and cook until reduced to half, about 10 minutes. Turn down the heat to low and add figs. Cook for 15 to 20 minutes, while spooning the juice over the figs, until the fruit is cooked and puffy.

TO SERVE: Place a scoop of ice cream on each of 4 serving plates. Press 2 to 3 figs into each scoop of ice cream and drizzle cooking syrup from figs over top.

ICE CREAM
1 cup/250 mL milk

1 cup/250 mL whipping cream

2 Tbsp/30 mL liquid honey

1 tsp/5 mL lavender blossoms

6 egg yolks

1 Tbsp/15 mL sugar

FIGS
½ cup/125 mL brown sugar

1½ cups/375 mL ruby port

½ cup/125 mL water

1 lb/450 g Black Mission figs, destemmed

Frozen PARFAIT with
Caramelized Nuts and Bourbon

. . . .

NUTS

¼ cup/60 mL walnuts

¼ cup/60 mL hazelnuts

¼ cup/60 mL almonds

⅔ cup/150 mL water

1 cup/250 mL sugar

¼ lemon, juice of

⅓ cup/75 mL liquid honey

SIMPLE SYRUP

¼ cup/60 mL sugar

¼ cup/60 mL water

PARFAIT

2 cups/500 mL whipping cream

8 egg yolks

¼ cup/60 mL Jack Daniel's
   bourbon

A PARFAIT IS A BASIC SABAYON (egg yolks and syrup) flavoured with nuts, orange or chocolate and finished with whipping cream. It is an easy way to make a frozen dessert, especially if you don't have an ice cream machine at home. You also can make the sabayon in a mixer using a whisk attachment. To heat the sabayon, use a small blowtorch (available from specialty cookware stores) and heat around the bowl evenly to avoid burning the eggs.

To create a little bit of a show, warm up 2 oz/60 mL of bourbon in a small saucepan and ignite it. Pour the flaming bourbon over the terrine slices.

Makes 4 servings

NUTS: Preheat the oven to 375°F/190°C. Spread out walnuts, hazelnuts and almonds on a cookie sheet and toast in the oven for about 7 minutes, stirring occasionally, until golden.

Combine water, sugar, lemon juice and honey in a saucepan on medium heat and bring to a boil. Cook for about 2 minutes, until the mixture turns a golden caramel colour. Stir in toasted nuts. Remove from the heat and stir very gently with a spoon.

Spread out the mixture on a sheet of parchment paper and allow it to cool. When the nut mixture is cold, place it in a food processor and crumble it gently.

SIMPLE SYRUP: Combine sugar and water in a saucepan on medium heat and bring to a boil. Remove from the heat and set aside.

PARFAIT: Line an 8 × 8 × 3-inch/750 mL terrine pan with plastic wrap.

Pour whipping cream into a kitchen mixer with a whisk attachment and whip until it forms firm peaks. Place whipped cream in a bowl, cover and refrigerate until needed.

Combine egg yolks and simple syrup in a stainless steel bowl placed over a saucepan of hot water on medium heat. Whisk the mixture without stopping for about 7 minutes. The temperature should remain below 160°F/70°C. Remove from the heat when the mixture becomes firm. Mix in the bourbon, using a spatula so the dessert stays foamy. Slowly and gently fold in whipped cream and caramelized nuts.

Transfer the parfait to the terrine pan, then freeze for 24 hours.

ASSEMBLY: Turn the terrine upside down and place it under hot running water for 30 seconds, making sure the parfait does not fall out. Place the terrine upside down on a cutting board; the parfait should now come out easily.

Transfer the frozen parfait to a plate and put it back in the freezer for 1 hour before serving.

TO SERVE: Slice the parfait with a knife warmed under hot running water and place on individual plates. Serve immediately.

FRUIT Pavlova

. . . .

MERINGUE

1 cup/250 mL berry sugar +
   1 tsp/5 mL for the cookie sheet

4 egg whites

Pinch of salt

½ tsp/2.5 mL lemon juice

1½ tsp/7.5 mL cornstarch

TOPPING

½ vanilla bean or 1 tsp/5 mL
   vanilla extract

2 cups/500 mL whipping cream

2 Tbsp/30 mL sugar

1 passion fruit

1 kiwi

1 cup/250 mL strawberries

½ cup/125 mL blueberries

½ cup/125 mL blackberries

½ cup/125 mL raspberries

COULIS

3 kiwis

2 Tbsp/30 mL sugar

½ orange, juice of

*T*HIS IS A VERY LIGHT DESSERT made with fresh berries or, in the winter, with exotic fruit such as mango, pineapple or kiwi. To get a nice smooth consistency, refrigerate the egg whites for a couple of hours before whipping them. You can make the meringue a day ahead and keep it at room temperature until needed.

Makes 4 servings

MERINGUE: Preheat the oven to 300°F/150°C. Line a cookie sheet with parchment paper. Sprinkle the 1 tsp/5 mL berry sugar over the parchment paper.

Place egg whites and a pinch of salt in a kitchen mixer with a whisk attachment. Whisk slowly for 1 minute, then increase the speed to high and whisk until egg whites have doubled in volume and are firm. Add lemon juice and mix for 30 seconds. Turn down the speed to low and mix for 2 minutes while slowly adding the remaining berry sugar and the cornstarch.

Use a tablespoon to make 4 meringues on the parchment paper. Bake in the oven for 30 minutes. Turn down the heat to 250°F/120°C and bake for 20 minutes, until tops are crisp. Remove meringues from the oven and allow to cool.

TOPPING: Cut vanilla bean in half lengthwise and scrape out half of the seeds. Set aside husk and remaining seeds for use in another recipe.

Place vanilla seeds and whipping cream in a kitchen mixer with a whisk attachment, and whip cream until firm. Add sugar, mix again and spoon the mixture into a pastry bag.

Cut passion fruit in half, then scoop out the flesh with a spoon. Peel kiwi and cut into 12 slices. Rinse berries and dry on paper towels.

COULIS: Peel kiwis and place in a blender with sugar and orange juice. Mix for 1 minute.

TO SERVE: Place each meringue on a serving plate, pipe whipped cream over it and top with assorted berries, passion fruit and kiwi. Serve coulis in a bowl on the side. Alternatively, pour a circle of coulis on each serving plate and place the pavlova on top of it.

Warm Soft-set Belgian
CHOCOLATE CAKE with Raspberries
and Peppermint Sauce
. . . .

SAUCE

1 cup/250 mL sugar

2 tsp/10 mL lemon juice

¾ cup/175 mL water

½ cup/125 mL fresh peppermint
   leaves

CAKE

1 Tbsp/15 mL melted butter

1 Tbsp/15 mL all-purpose flour

5½ oz/155 g Belgian dark chocolate,
   finely chopped

5 oz/140 g butter, room temperature,
   in ½-inch/1-cm cubes

5 eggs

1 Tbsp/15 mL sugar

2 oz/60 g all-purpose flour
   (about ½ cup/125 mL)

⅔ cup/150 mL raspberries

I LIKE TO FINISH A MEAL with a warm chocolate dessert. The idea of this dish is to serve the cake half cooked, so that when you take a forkful of the cake, the chocolate will run onto the plate and you can see the raspberries inside. The effect is sinfully delicious.

You will have to be very precise with your cooking time because you don't want to overcook the cake. If you are using a convection oven, you may have to reduce your cooking time by one minute or so. To save time, you can make the cake batter a day ahead and refrigerate it overnight.

For variety, replace the raspberries and the peppermint sauce with the zest of 1 orange and a dark chocolate sauce (page 168), with 1½ tsp/7.5 mL freshly ground coffee and a butterscotch sauce (page 168) or with pieces of 2 passion fruit plus a citrus coulis (page 167).

Makes 4 servings

SAUCE: Combine sugar, lemon juice and water in a saucepan on medium heat, then boil for 2 minutes. Turn off the heat and add half of the peppermint. Cover the pan with a lid and allow the mixture to infuse and cool. Strain the sauce through a sieve into a blender, discarding the solids. Add the remaining peppermint and mix for 1 minute. Let the sauce cool, place it in a covered container and refrigerate until needed, up to 1 day.

CAKE: Brush the insides of 4 ramekins, each 2½ inches/6 cm in diameter, with the 1 Tbsp/15 mL of melted butter. Sprinkle with the 1 Tbsp/15 mL of flour, turn upside down and tap gently to remove any excess.

Place chocolate and butter in a stainless steel bowl over a saucepan of hot water on medium heat, then mix gently with a wooden spoon until melted. Remove from the heat and allow the mixture to cool for a few minutes.

Place eggs and sugar in a kitchen mixer with a paddle attachment and mix until sugar is well incorporated and eggs are pale in colour. Slowly add the egg mixture to the melted chocolate, stirring constantly. Slowly add flour, stirring to incorporate it.

Fill the ramekins half full with the chocolate mixture. Place 4 raspberries in each, then add more chocolate mixture until the ramekins are three quarters full. Place the ramekins in the refrigerator for 2 hours.

Preheat the oven to 375°F/190°C. Bake the cakes in the oven for 12 to 14 minutes, until soft set. Remove the cakes from the oven and cool. Turn the ramekins upside down and use a spatula to remove the cakes very gently.

TO SERVE: Place the cakes on 4 warmed serving plates. Serve the sauce in a sauceboat on the side.

Black and White
CHOCOLATE Tower
. . . .

WHAT A DECADENT, easy-to-make chocolate dessert. For moulds, we use clean PVC plumbing pipe, 2 inches/5 cm in diameter and 2½ inches/6 cm in length, lined with waxed paper so the mousse doesn't stick. This resulting tower looks impressive, especially served with any fruit coulis. If you prefer, you can also make this dessert in ramekins. Substitute crème de menthe or rum for the Grand Marnier, if you like.

You can prepare this dessert a week in advance and keep it in the freezer in moulds until needed. Wrap the moulds in plastic wrap to protect the chocolate from taking on any bad tastes. You can also serve this dish with a coulis or a vanilla sauce.

Makes 4 servings

DARK CHOCOLATE MOUSSE: Melt dark chocolate with milk in a stainless steel bowl over a saucepan of hot water on medium heat, stirring constantly. Remove chocolate mixture from the heat and whisk in egg yolks, one at a time. Add cognac and slowly fold in the whipped cream.

WHITE CHOCOLATE MOUSSE: Place gelatin leaves in a bowl with cold water and cover. Allow to soak for 5 minutes, until soft.

Melt white chocolate with milk in a stainless steel bowl over a saucepan of hot water on medium heat, stirring constantly. Remove chocolate mixture from the heat. Remove soaked gelatin leaves from water, squeeze gently to remove excess water and whisk in. Add Grand Marnier and slowly fold in the whipped cream. Allow to rest at room temperature for 5 minutes.

CHOUX PASTRY: Preheat the oven to 375°F/190°C. Line a cookie sheet with parchment paper.

Place water, butter and salt in a saucepan. Bring to a boil on medium heat, stirring occasionally with a spoon, until butter melts. Remove from the heat and add flour all at once. Stir until thoroughly mixed.

Return to the heat and cook for 1 to 2 minutes, or until batter no longer sticks to the spoon or the sides of the saucepan.

continued overleaf >

DARK CHOCOLATE MOUSSE
3 oz/85 g semi-sweet dark chocolate, finely chopped

3 Tbsp/45 mL milk

2 egg yolks

1½ tsp/7.5 mL cognac

¾ cup/175 mL whipping cream, whipped until firm

WHITE CHOCOLATE MOUSSE
2 leaves gelatin

3 oz/85 g white chocolate, finely chopped

3 Tbsp/45 mL milk

1 Tbsp/15 mL Grand Marnier or other orange liqueur

¾ cup/175 mL whipping cream, whipped until firm

CHOUX PASTRY
½ cup/125 mL water

1½ oz/45 g butter

Pinch of salt

2¾ oz/78 g all-purpose flour

2 eggs

Transfer batter to the bowl of an electric mixer. Add eggs and mix, using leaf beaters, for 2 minutes, until batter is smooth, soft and shiny.

Spoon batter into a pastry bag fitted with a small round tip. Pipe four 6-inch/15-cm zigzag shapes onto the prepared cookie sheet. Bake for 10 to 15 minutes, until pastries are golden brown. Cool on a wire rack.

ASSEMBLY: For moulds for the towers, use clean PVC plumbing pipe or ramekins.

Place a strip of waxed paper 6½ × 2½ inches/17 × 6 cm inside each mould so that the chocolate won't stick when it sets. Set the moulds on a tray lined with parchment paper. Fill each mould with alternating layers of dark chocolate mousse and white chocolate mousse. To create a marble effect, mix the mousses gently with a bamboo skewer. Cover the entire tray and the moulds with plastic wrap. Refrigerate overnight.

TO SERVE: Unmould the chocolate mousses on separate serving plates, remove the waxed paper and garnish with a choux pastry.

BASICS

Stocks

· · · · · · · · · ·

STOCK is the basic and most important ingredient used to make a sauce or soup, and I strongly recommend that you learn how to make your own. Artificial stock in the form of powder or paste or cubes is a very poor substitute for the real thing. As an alternative, you may be able to find pre-packaged home-made stock in some specialty stores.

In this cookbook, I provide two brown stock recipes that you can use as a basic method for making many others. Try lamb, beef, venison, duck, pigeon and so on.

Stock should not be seasoned, as the salt and pepper becomes too strong-tasting when the liquid is reduced.

Once made, stock will keep in a refrigerator for up to 2 days. You can also pour stock into ice-cube trays and freeze it. Once frozen, place the cubes in a resealable plastic bag and keep them in the freezer for later use. Frozen, the stock will keep for 4 to 5 weeks.

MUSSEL JUS

2 lbs/900 g mussels
1 Tbsp/15 mL butter
2 shallots, thinly sliced
2 cloves garlic, thinly sliced
2 sprigs fresh parsley, roughly
    chopped
1 bay leaf
1¼ cups/360 mL Sauvignon Blanc

Wash mussels, making sure to remove and discard their beards.

Melt butter in a stockpot on medium heat and sauté shallots for 2 minutes, until translucent. Add garlic, parsley, bay leaf, wine and mussels. Cover the pot with a lid and cook on high heat for 2 minutes, until the mussels open. Use a slotted spoon to remove the mussels. Discard the shells but reserve the meat for use in a salad or fish soup. Allow the mussel jus to cool, then strain it through a sieve and discard any solids.

The mussel jus is now ready. Refrigerate it until needed or freeze for later use.

Makes 1¼ cups/310 mL

FISH STOCK

2 lbs/900 g assorted fish bones
    (sole, snapper, salmon, halibut)
1 Tbsp/15 mL olive oil
1 large onion, thinly sliced
½ bulb fennel, thinly sliced
1 leek, thinly sliced
1 stalk celery, thinly sliced
1 carrot, thinly sliced
2 cloves garlic, thinly sliced
1 sprig fresh parsley
2 bay leaves
Pinch of fennel seeds
2 cups/500 mL Chardonnay

Rinse the fish bones under cold running water.

Heat olive oil in a stockpot on medium-low heat, then sauté onion, fennel, leek, celery, carrot and garlic for 5 minutes, until onion is translucent. Add fish bones, parsley, bay leaves, fennel seeds and wine. Cook for 2 minutes, then add enough water to cover the bones. Continue cooking until stock starts to simmer, then turn down the heat to low and simmer for 40 minutes.

Skim off and discard the fat and foam. Turn off the heat and let the stock infuse for 1 hour.

Strain the stock through a sieve, then discard the bones and solids.

The stock is now ready. Refrigerate until needed or freeze for later use.

Makes 8 cups/2 L

WHITE CHICKEN STOCK

2¼ lbs/1 kg chicken bones

3 oz/85 g chicken feet

12 cups/3 L water

1 carrot, in ¾-inch/2-cm cubes

1 onion, in ¾-inch/2-cm cubes

1 tomato, in ¾-inch/2-cm cubes

1 stalk celery, in ¾-inch/2-cm cubes

1 small leek, in ½-inch/1-cm cubes

2 cloves garlic

¼ bunch fresh parsley

1 sprig fresh thyme

2 bay leaves

2 cloves

Place chicken bones and feet in a stockpot. Add enough cold water to cover, and bring to a boil on medium heat. Turn down the heat to low and simmer gently for 1 minute. Drain and discard all the water from the stockpot, then add the 12 cups/3 L of water to the chicken.

Add carrot, onion, tomato, celery, leek, garlic, parsley, thyme, bay leaves and cloves to the stockpot. Return the stockpot to the stove on medium heat and simmer for 2½ hours.

Skim off and discard the fat and foam. Turn off the heat and

let the stock infuse for 1 hour. Strain through a sieve and discard the bones and solids.

The stock is now ready. Refrigerate until needed or freeze for later use.

Makes 9 cups/2.25 L

VEGETABLE STOCK

2 Tbsp/30 mL olive oil

1 carrot, in ¼-inch/5-mm cubes

4 shallots, in ¼-inch/5-mm cubes

2 cloves garlic, in ¼-inch/ 5-mm cubes

2 tomatoes, in ¼-inch/5-mm cubes

1 small leek, in ¼-inch/5-mm cubes

2 stalks celery, in ¼-inch/5-mm cubes

½ bunch fresh parsley

1 sprig fresh thyme

1 bay leaf

8 cups/2 L water

You can use this stock in place of water in any recipe, especially vegetarian ones. You can also use it in recipes that call for meat or fish stock, when you want a lighter consistency.

Heat olive oil in a stockpot on medium heat. Add carrot, shallots, garlic, tomatoes, leek, celery, parsley, thyme and bay leaf. Sauté for 2 minutes, until shallots are translucent. Add water, season to taste with salt

and pepper, then simmer on medium heat for 25 minutes.

Remove from the heat and allow the stock to cool. Strain through a sieve and discard any solids.

The stock is now ready. Refrigerate until needed or freeze for later use.

Makes 5 cups/1.25 L

COURT BOUILLON

1 onion, thinly sliced

1 carrot, thinly sliced

1 stalk celery, thinly sliced

2 shallots, thinly sliced

2 cloves garlic, crushed

2 sprigs fresh parsley

1 sprig fresh thyme

2 bay leaves

2 Tbsp/30 mL rock salt

1 tsp/5 mL crushed white pepper

¾ cup/175 mL white vinegar

3 cups/750 mL Chardonnay

24 cups/6 L water

Combine all court bouillon ingredients in a stockpot on medium heat. Bring to a boil and cook for 10 minutes. Strain bouillon into a clean bowl, discarding solids. Fill the sink one quarter full with cold water and ice cubes, then place the bowl of stock in the sink to cool quickly. Pour cooled stock into resealable plastic bags, seal and freeze for up to 1 month.

Makes 24 cups/6 L

BROWN CHICKEN STOCK

2¼ lbs/1 kg chicken bones

5 oz/140 g chicken feet

1 carrot, in 1-inch/2.5-cm cubes

1 onion, in 1-inch/2.5-cm cubes

1 tomato, in 1-inch/2.5-cm cubes

1 stalk celery, in 1-inch/2.5-cm cubes

3 cloves garlic

1 sprig fresh thyme

2 bay leaves

2 Tbsp/30 mL tomato paste

12 cups/3 L water

Preheat the oven to 375°F/ 190°C. Arrange the chicken bones and feet in a roasting pan and roast for 45 minutes.

Add carrot, onion, tomato, celery, garlic, thyme, bay leaves and tomato paste, and toss gently. Roast for 15 more minutes, or until vegetables are golden brown.

Use a slotted spoon to transfer the contents of the pan to a stockpot.

Drain and discard fat from the roasting pan. Place the roasting pan on the stove on medium heat, add 1 cup/ 250 mL of the water and deglaze the pan. Pour the liquid into the stockpot and add the remaining water. Simmer (do not boil) on low heat for 3½ hours. Make sure the bones are always covered with water, adding more if necessary.

Skim off and discard the fat and foam. Allow the stock to cool, then strain through a sieve and discard the bones and solids.

The stock is now ready. Refrigerate until needed or freeze for later use.

Makes 9 cups/2.25 L

BROWN VEAL STOCK

2½ lbs/1.2 kg veal bones,
   in 2-inch/5-cm lengths

5 oz/140 g beef tendons

1 carrot, in 1-inch/2.5-cm cubes

1 onion, in 1-inch/2.5-cm cubes

1 stalk celery, in 1-inch/2.5-cm cubes

2 cloves garlic

1 sprig fresh thyme

2 bay leaves

2 Tbsp/30 mL tomato paste

12 cups/3 L water

Preheat the oven to 375°F/ 190°C. Arrange the bones and tendons in a roasting pan and roast for about 45 minutes, until they turn a nice golden colour.

Add carrot, onion, celery, garlic, thyme, bay leaves and tomato paste, and toss gently. Roast for 15 more minutes.

Use a slotted spoon to transfer the contents of the roasting pan to a stockpot.

Drain and discard the fat from the roasting pan. Place the roasting pan on the stove on medium heat, add 1 cup/ 250 mL of the water and de-glaze the pan. Pour the liquid into the stockpot and add the remaining water. Simmer (do not boil) on low heat for 4 hours. Make sure the bones are always covered with water, adding more if necessary. Skim off and discard the fat and foam.

Strain the stock through a sieve and discard the bones and solids. Return the stock to the pot on medium heat and cook for about 1 hour, until the liquid is reduced to 4 cups/1 L.

Fill the sink one quarter full with cold water and ice cubes, and place the stockpot in the sink to cool quickly.

The stock is now ready. Refrigerate for up to 5 days until needed or freeze for later use.

Makes 4 cups/1 L

Vinaigrettes

......

*T*HESE are basic recipes that are easy to prepare and have many uses. I personally like to use a blender to give my vinaigrettes a really nice smooth consistency. Vinaigrettes can be made up to 1 week ahead and then kept in the refrigerator.

BASIL AND OLIVE OIL VINAIGRETTE

½ sun-dried tomato

⅓ cup/75 mL balsamic vinegar

2 cloves garlic, quartered

1 shallot, quartered

1 Tbsp/15 mL Dijon mustard

1 cup/250 mL extra-virgin olive oil

¼ cup/60 mL water

2 Tbsp/30 mL chopped fresh basil

Place sun-dried tomato and balsamic vinegar in a bowl. Cover and let soak overnight at room temperature. Drain the sun-dried tomato and reserve the balsamic vinegar. Cut the sun-dried tomato into small cubes.

Remove and discard the centre germ from garlic. Place garlic, balsamic vinegar, shallot and Dijon mustard in a blender and mix briefly. With the blender running, slowly add olive oil. Once the consistency becomes thick, add water and mix for 10 seconds. Stir in basil and sun-dried tomato and season to taste with salt and pepper.

Will keep in a tightly covered container in the refrigerator for up to a week.

Makes 1 ½ cups/375 mL

CITRUS VINAIGRETTE

1 cup/250 mL fresh orange juice

1 lemon, juice of

½ grapefruit, juice of

1½ tsp/7.5 mL Dijon mustard

2 Tbsp/30 mL rice vinegar

⅓ cup/75 mL extra-virgin olive oil

¼ cup/60 mL vegetable oil

1 Tbsp/15 ml fresh Italian flat-leaf parsley

¼ tsp/1 mL Italian cracked black pepper or crushed black pepper

1 Tbsp/15 mL chopped shallot

Place orange juice in a saucepan on medium heat and cook until reduced to one quarter, about 4 minutes. Remove from the heat and allow to cool.

Pour reduced orange juice, lemon juice and grapefruit juice into a blender. Add Dijon mustard and rice vinegar, then mix briefly.

In a bowl, mix together olive and vegetable oils. With the blender running, slowly add the combined oils to the citrus juices. Add parsley, black pepper and shallot, then mix briefly. Season to taste with salt.

Will keep in a tightly covered container in the refrigerator for up to a week.

Makes 1 cup/250 mL

SOY AND SESAME SEED VINAIGRETTE

1½ tsp/7.5 mL sesame seeds

1½ tsp/7.5 mL grainy mustard

1½ tsp/7.5 mL liquid honey

¼ cup/60 mL rice vinegar

¼ cup/60 mL soy sauce

½ cup/125 mL sesame oil

¼ cup/60 mL vegetable oil

Place sesame seeds in a frying pan on medium heat and toast for about 1 minute, until golden. Transfer to a plate and allow to cool.

Place grainy mustard, honey, rice vinegar and soy sauce in a blender and mix briefly.

Mix together sesame oil and vegetable oil in a bowl. With the blender running, slowly add the combined oils to the mustard mixture. Add toasted sesame seeds and season to taste with freshly ground black pepper.

Will keep in a tightly covered container in the refrigerator for up to a week.

Makes 1 ¼ cups/310 mL

PEANUT VINAIGRETTE

¼ cup/60 mL smooth unsweetened
    peanut butter

½ cup/125 mL rice vinegar

1 Tbsp/15 mL pickled ginger

¼ cup/60 mL sesame oil

¼ cup/60 mL vegetable oil

1 lime, juice of

¼ tsp/1 mL sambal oelek

Place peanut butter, rice vinegar and pickled ginger in a blender. Mix for 1 minute.

Mix together sesame oil and vegetable oil in a bowl. With the blender running, slowly add the combined oils to the peanut butter mixture. Add lime juice and sambal oelek and mix briefly. Season to taste with salt and pepper.

Will keep in a tightly covered container in the refrigerator for up to a week.

Makes 1 ¼ cups/310 mL

TOMATO VINAIGRETTE

2 Roma tomatoes

¼ red onion

¼ stalk celery, sliced

¼ cup/60 mL red wine vinegar

¼ tsp/1 mL brown sugar

¾ cup/175 mL vegetable oil

1½ tsp/7.5 mL chopped fresh Italian
    flat-leaf parsley

1½ tsp/7.5 mL Worcestershire sauce

2 drops Tabasco

¼ cup/60 mL Chardonnay

Peel and cut tomatoes and onion into ½-inch/1-cm cubes. Place tomatoes, onion and celery in a food processor. Add red wine vinegar, brown sugar and season to taste with salt and pepper. Mix briefly. Add vegetable oil, parsley, Worcestershire sauce, Tabasco and wine, then mix briefly. The vinaigrette should be chunky.

Will keep in a tightly covered container in the refrigerator for up to 5 days.

Makes 1½ cups/375 mL

LOBSTER OIL AND
CHIPOTLE VINAIGRETTE

Lobster oil is an infusion made from fresh lobster shells, vegetables and tomatoes. At The Cannery, we make our own signature lobster oil. It is also available at fine food stores.

1½ tsp/7.5 mL Dijon mustard

¼ cup/60 mL sherry vinegar or red
    wine vinegar

¾ tsp/4 mL dried chipotle pepper

1½ tsp/7.5 mL chopped shallot

½ cup/125 mL lobster oil

3 Tbsp/45 mL vegetable oil

1½ tsp/7.5 mL water

1 tsp/5 mL chopped fresh tarragon

Place Dijon mustard, sherry vinegar, chipotle pepper and shallot in a blender. Mix for 30 seconds.

Mix together lobster oil and vegetable oil in a bowl. With the blender running, slowly add the combined oils to the mustard mixture and mix for 2 minutes. Add water and mix briefly. Stir in tarragon, then season to taste with salt and pepper.

Will keep in a tightly covered container in the refrigerator for up to a week.

Makes ¾ cup/180 mL

CREAMY MUSSEL VINAIGRETTE

2 cups/500 mL mussel jus (page 162)

1 clove garlic

1 shallot, quartered

1½ tsp/7.5 mL Dijon mustard

¼ cup/60 mL red wine vinegar

¼ tsp/1 mL freshly ground black
    pepper

¾ cup/175 mL extra-virgin olive oil

1½ tsp/7.5 mL chopped fresh
    tarragon

Place mussel jus in a saucepan on medium heat and cook until reduced to ¼ cup/60 mL, about 14 minutes. Remove from the heat and allow to cool.

Remove and discard the centre germ from garlic. Place garlic, shallot, Dijon mustard, red wine vinegar and black pepper in a blender and mix briefly. With the blender running, slowly add olive oil. If the consistency becomes too thick, add a little water and mix briefly. Add tarragon, then season to taste with salt and pepper.

Will keep in a tightly covered container in the refrigerator for up to a week.

Makes 1½ cups/310 mL

Coulis

· · · · · · · · · ·

A COULIS is a combination of fruit and sugar, and it is a delicious complement to a dessert. Use ripe fresh fruit, or if you have to use frozen fruit, try to buy fruit that is IQF (individually quick frozen). You can also cook the fruit for a coulis so that it will keep in the refrigerator for a couple of days.

You can also add a touch of Grand Marnier or Cointreau.

BERRY COULIS

Serve this coulis over chocolate cake, ice cream or yogurt. Raspberries and strawberries are most commonly used to make this coulis, but try blueberries or blackberries when they are in season.

½ cup/125 mL sugar
1 cup/250 mL water
1 lb/450 g raspberries or strawberries
1 tsp/5 mL lemon juice

Combine sugar and water in a saucepan on medium heat and bring to a boil. Add berries and lemon juice and cook for 2 minutes, until the fruit is completely cooked.

Transfer to a blender and mix for 1 minute. Strain through a sieve into a bowl and discard solids. Allow to cool. Cover and refrigerate for up to 5 days, or freeze coulis until needed.

Makes 2 cups/500 mL

FRUIT COULIS

This coulis of fresh fruit must be used on the same day it is made, otherwise it will turn brown. Serve it with a baked tart, over ice cream or as a dipping sauce for fresh fruit such as pineapple, mango and banana.

1 lb/450 g mango or apricot or kiwi or pineapple
⅓ cup/75 mL water
½ cup/125 mL ice cubes
½ cup/125 mL sugar

Peel fruit, remove and discard pits or cores, and cut into chunks. Place in a blender with water, ice cubes and sugar. Mix for 1 minute. Add water if necessary, depending on the thickness of the coulis. Refrigerate for up to 6 hours but do not freeze.

Makes 2 cups/500 mL

CITRUS COULIS

Serve this coulis with cheesecake, pavlova or summer berry terrine.

2 lemons
2 limes
2 oranges
1 grapefruit
1 cup/250 mL sugar
1 Tbsp/15 mL orange marmalade
2 Tbsp/30 mL cornstarch
2 Tbsp/30 mL water
2 Tbsp/30 mL Grand Marnier or other orange liqueur

Cut lemons, limes, oranges and grapefruit in half. Extract juice from them without squeezing too much, or you will get a bitter taste from the skin. Strain the combined juices into a bowl.

Place sugar and half of the combined juices in a saucepan on medium heat, and cook for 2 minutes. Slowly pour in the remaining juice. Turn down the heat to low, stir in the marmalade and cook for 1 minute, whisking constantly.

Mix together cornstarch and water in a cup. Pour the mixture slowly into the coulis, whisking constantly, and cook for 2 minutes. Stir in Grand Marnier. Transfer to a clean bowl and allow to cool. Cover and refrigerate for up to 5 days but do not freeze.

Makes 2 cups/500 mL

Dessert Sauces

. . . .

DARK CHOCOLATE SAUCE

This is a sauce for chocolate lovers! Serve it as a chocolate fondue or pour it over vanilla ice cream or frozen cake.

1½ cups/375 mL finely chopped
   good-quality dark chocolate
1 cup/250 mL milk
½ cup/125 mL whipping cream
1 orange, zest of

Place dark chocolate, milk and whipping cream in a stainless steel bowl over a saucepan of hot water on low heat. Stir constantly while the chocolate melts. The texture should be smooth and shiny. Add the orange zest.

Transfer sauce to a clean bowl, cover and set aside until needed. It will keep in the refrigerator for a few days. To reheat this sauce before serving, warm it in a microwave on low power or in a saucepan over low heat.

Makes 2 cups/500 mL

BUTTERSCOTCH SAUCE

Serve this sauce with chocolate cake or any dessert made with nuts or honey.

4 oz/115 g butter
⅓ cup/75 mL water
½ lb/225 g sugar
   (about 1½ cups/375 mL)
1 cup/250 mL whipping cream

Cut butter into ½-inch/1-cm cubes and leave at room temperature for 30 minutes.

Combine water and sugar in a saucepan on medium heat and cook, stirring constantly, for about 8 minutes, until the mixture turns a golden caramel. Turn down the heat to low and slowly stir in butter. Turn off the heat and whisk for a few minutes. Slowly stir in the whipping cream.

Transfer to a clean container and allow to cool. Cover and refrigerate up to 7 days.

To use the sauce, warm it in the microwave on low power, for 1 minute until soft.

Makes 2 cups/500 mL

CRÈME ANGLAISE

Use this classic sauce with any dessert cake.

½ vanilla bean or ½ tsp/
   2.5 mL vanilla extract
1½ cups/375 mL milk
⅔ cup/150 mL whipping cream
7 egg yolks
½ cup/125 mL sugar

Cut vanilla bean in half lengthwise, then scrape out seeds with the tip of a knife. Save seeds and husk.

Combine milk, whipping cream, vanilla bean husk and seeds in a saucepan on medium heat and bring to a boil. Remove from the heat, cover with a lid and let vanilla infuse for 5 minutes.

Place egg yolks in a bowl and slowly add sugar while whisking for about 2 minutes, until sugar is well incorporated and the mixture is white. While stirring for 1 minute, slowly pour in half of the warm milk mixture, stirring constantly. Stir in the remaining warm milk mixture.

Transfer to a heavy-bottomed saucepan on low heat and cook for 5 minutes, stirring constantly with a spoon, until the mixture thickens slightly. Turn off the heat when the temperature reaches about 165°F/ 75°C. To check if the sauce is done, dip the wooden spoon into the sauce, take it out and draw a line across the back of it with your finger. If the line stays put, the sauce is done. If the line runs, the sauce needs more cooking.

When the sauce is done, transfer it to a clean bowl placed over a bowl of ice water, to stop the cooking. Stir for a couple of minutes as it cools. Allow to cool until it becomes totally cold. Cover the bowl with plastic wrap to prevent a crust from forming and keep in the refrigerator for up to 4 days.

Makes 2 cups/500 mL

Special Occasion Menus

. . . .

NEW YEAR'S EVE

Appetizer 1: Cured Quebec Foie Gras with Smoked Goose Breast

Appetizer 2: Maple Syrup–glazed Smoked Sablefish with Shallot Compote and Frisée Lettuce with Hazelnut Vinaigrette

Soup: Creamy Mussel and Saffron Soup

Main course: Mushroom-crusted Beef Tenderloin with Gorgonzola Mashed Potatoes and Red Wine Sauce

Dessert: Black and White Chocolate Tower

VALENTINE'S DAY

Appetizer: Ahi Tuna Gravlax, Accented with Green Cardamom and Chuka Wakame

Soup: Celeriac and Smoked Black Cod Potage

Main course: Giant Scallops and Seared Foie Gras with Fig Molasses

Dessert: Blood Orange Crème Brûlée

EASTER

Appetizer: Pan-roasted Mussels and Clams with Sizzling Brown Butter and Capers

Soup: Fish Soup, Mediterranean-style

Main course: Smoked Rack of Lamb with Confit Vegetables and Whipped Chickpeas

Dessert: Pineapple and Lemon Cheesecake

MOTHER'S DAY

Appetizer: Dungeness Crab Cakes with Nori Mayonnaise and Jicama Salad

Soup: Chilled Cucumber and Dill Soup with Preserved Salmon Roe

Main course: Red Snapper "en Papillote" with Thai Basil

Dessert: Thai Mango Clafoutis

THANKSGIVING

Appetizer: Pacific Salmon Roe with Wild Rice Galettes and Lemon-Dill Crème Fraîche

Soup: Lobster Bisque

Main course: Roasted Capon with Caramelized Root Vegetables

Dessert: Baked Apples with Toasted Pistachio Crème Fraîche

CHRISTMAS

Appetizer: Scallop Carpaccio with Ginger–Lemon Grass Oil and Tobiko

Soup: Creamy Beach Oyster Soup

Main course: Veal Cutlets and Lobster with Creamy Tarragon Sauce

Dessert: Frozen Parfait with Caramelized Nuts and Bourbon

AN ASIAN-THEMED DINNER

Appetizer: Spawn-on-Kelp Tempura with Soy-Ginger Sauce and Daikon Salad

Soup: South Asian Salmon Soup

Main course: Halibut Steamed with Lapsang Souchong Tea, Sweet and Sour Sauce

Dessert: Fresh fruit platter

SUMMER BUFFET

Appetizers 1: Seafood Salad, South Asian–style; Poached Spot Prawns with Lobster Oil Mayonnaise; Smoked Salmon and Pickled Cucumber in a Vietnamese Salad Roll with Tamarind Sauce

Appetizers 2: Pan-roasted Mussels and Clams with Sizzling Brown Butter and Capers; Neon Squid Saté-style with Peanut Sauce; Rosemary-glazed Corn on the Cob

Desserts: Fruit Pavlova; Summer Berry Terrine; Strawberries with Fresh Mint and White Balsamic Reduction

Index

. . . .

Ahi tuna gravlax accented with green cardamom and chuka wakame salad, 22–23
apples, baked, 139
apricots, in fruit coulis, 167
apricot tart with hazelnut crust, 142–43
Arctic char, cedar planked, 72
artichokes, Chinese, risotto, 128
asparagus, crab rolls with, 101
avocado soup, chilled, with crab, 65
avocado-tomato salsa, 91

Bacon, smoked, and green lentil soup, 59
bacon and celery mashed potatoes, 77
baked apples with toasted pistachio crème fraîche, 139
baked cherry tomatoes, onion and goat cheese on puff pastry with tomato-basil sauce, 35
balsamic and port figs, roasted, 127
balsamic reductions, 12, 146
Bartlett pear and toasted almond tart, 145
basil, snapper "en papillote" with, 86
basil, cockles with chili, garlic and, 31
basil and prosciutto king crab tempura, 101
basil soup, tomato, black bean and, 58
basmati rice, cardamom, 82
batter(s), 26, 42
    beer, 89, 99
    tempura, 40, 43, 101
bean(s)
    black, Chinese fermented, with crab, 98
    black, soup, Roma tomato, basil and, 58
    Chinese long, in green papaya salad, 102
    green, 96–97
    mung, with curry oil–roasted tofu, 129
bean sprouts and green onions, 109
beef short ribs, honey-barbecued, 122–23
beef tenderloin, mushroom crusted, 118–19
Belgian endives and walnuts, 48–49
berries
    berry coulis, 167
    fruit Pavlova, 154
    raspberries with chocolate cake, 156–57
    raspberry sauce, 84

strawberries with mint and balsamic reduction, 146
summer berry relish, 72
summer berry terrine, 137
black and white chocolate tower, 159–60
blackened swordfish with mild creole sauce and rosemary-roasted sweet potatoes, 93
blood orange crème brûlée, 148–49
bok choy, sautéed, 83
bouillon, court, 163
bouquet garni, 15
bourbon parfait, frozen, 152–53
bread, toasted, with roasted tomatoes, 12
brill fillets, cornmeal-crusted, 91
brownies, dark chocolate, with nuts, 140
butter clams with mussel vinaigrette and wild mushroom fricassée, 38

Cake, warm Belgian Chocolate, 156–57
capon, roasted, 117
caramelized nuts, 152
caramelized root vegetables, 117
cardamom, tuna gravlax with, 22–23
cardamom basmati rice, 82
carpaccio, scallop, 21
carpaccio, sockeye salmon, 11
cedar-planked Arctic char with summer berry relish, 72
celeriac and smoked black cod potage, 62
celery and bacon mashed potatoes, 77
cheesecake, pineapple and lemon, 147
cheese(s). *See under individual names*
chervil-arugula-mesclun salad, 127
chicken stock, brown, 164
chicken stock, white, 163
chickpeas, whipped, 112
chili, cockles with garlic, basil, and, 31
chili mayonnaise, 42
chilled cucumber and dill soup with preserved salmon roe, 61
chilled avocado soup with Dungeness crabmeat and jalapeño sorbet, 65

chilled Nova Scotia lobster and crispy pickled cucumbers with dill and lemon balm cream sauce, 92
chipotle and lobster oil vinaigrette, 166
chipotle, corn and garlic soup with, 66
chive crème fraîche, 90
chocolate
    brownies, dark, with nuts, 140
    cake, Belgian, 156–57
    mousse, dark, 159
    mousse, white, 159
    mousse, white, and fig, 134
    sauce, dark, 168
    tower, black and white, 159–60
chuka wakame salad, 22–23
chutney, tomato, 82
clafoutis, Thai mango, 138
clam(s)
    butter, with mussel vinaigrette, 38
    chowder, 54
    Manila, in "pot-au-feu," 106
    Manila, in seafood salad, 15
    Manila, pan-roasted, with mussels, 27
    Manila, sautéed with scallops and mussels, 29
    Manila, soup with curry and sea asparagus, 63
    razor, pan-fried panko-coated, 39
cockles, sautéed with chili, garlic and basil, 31
cod
    grey, battered, 89
    ling, in "pot-au-feu," 106
    ling, with truffle risotto, 107
    smoked black, and celeriac potage, 62
    tongue, fritters, 99
coleslaw, smoked herring and pecan, 39
compote, lentil, 115
compote, shallot, 37
confit, rabbit legs, 127
confit, vegetables, 112
corn and elephant garlic soup with chipotle pepper, 66
cornmeal-crusted brill fillets with avocado-tomato salsa, 91
corn on the cob, rosemary-glazed, 122
corn tortilla cups, blue, 65